STO ✓

PAINTER OF THE WILD WEST

FREDERIC REMINGTON

Born:

October 1, 1861

Died:

December 26, 1909

PAINTER OF
THE WILD WEST

FREDERIC REMINGTON

by ROBIN McKOWN

JULIAN MESSNER, INC.   NEW YORK

Published by Julian Messner, Inc.
8 West 40 Street, New York 18

Published simultaneously in Canada
by The Copp Clark Publishing Co. Limited

Printed in the United States of America

Library of Congress Catalog Card No. 59-7014

FOR

CLAUDINE BISIAUX

ACKNOWLEDGMENTS

A great deal of credit for my understanding of Frederic Remington as a person is due to the citizens of Canton, New York, to whom I am indebted for their hospitality and their reminiscences during my stay there. I mention particularly Atwood **Manley**, former editor of the *Plaindealer*, whose grandfather, G. B. Manley, in 1873 bought this paper (then the *Plain Dealer*) from Colonel Seth Remington; Andrew K. Peters, Librarian of St. Lawrence University, whose sympathy with a researcher's problems was an education in itself; the gracious Librarian of the Canton Library, Mrs. Phyllis Clark; Mrs. Nina Smithers, the devoted and capable Historian of St. Lawrence County; and Sheriff Henry Denner, whose lake-captain father used to fish with Remington on Chippewa Bay.

Another debt of gratitude is due to David F. Lane of the Watertown, New York, *Daily Times*, who has himself done many excellent articles about Remington, and who went to considerable trouble to furnish me the data I requested of him. I also wish to express my appreciation for the assistance of Stewart Klonis of the New York Art Students League; Miss Marian Brickey of the Ogdensburg Public Library; Miss Hannah Egert, also of Ogdensburg, whose father was a friend of the artist; and Miss Ursula Hornbrook, Curator of the Remington Art Memorial.

My appreciation, too, to the New York Public Library and its staff, who have made available a large amount of Remington material, including eighteen massive scrapbooks in which the artist's work has been divided into categories—Cowboys and Sheepman; Indian Campaigns; U. S. Army; Hunting and Fishing; Spanish War; Mexico; Canada, etc.—and the excellent Merle Johnson collection of books illustrated by Remington; to the New York Historical Society Library; and to the Metropolitan Museum Library, whose files include the five scrapbooks carefully prepared by Helen Card.

Finally, I am grateful to Robert Taft, a Kansas University professor whom I never knew and who died two years ago, but whose fine scholarship is evident in his chapter on "Remington in Kansas" in his excellent *Artists and Illustrators of the Old West: 1850-1900*. It is a great loss that he did not live to complete the definitive biography of Frederic Remington that he contemplated.

ROBIN McKOWN

PAINTER OF THE WILD WEST

FREDERIC REMINGTON

It was a fight to death.

The two of them rolled over and over on the grassy turf in a stranglehold, hands clutching out wildly, feet kicking in the air, their faces twisted in the passion of battle. Then, finally, one was on top, the other pinned firmly to the ground.

"Give up, Crazy Horse?" shouted the victor triumphantly.

"Oh, all right. Now let me go."

"Not yet. Say, 'Please let me go, General Frederic Remington.'"

"I will not." It was a feeble but defiant gasp.

"You won't?" Suddenly the "General" was brandishing a pair of deadly shears. "Then I'm going to scalp you."

"Hey, stop that." There was a frantic struggle from "Crazy Horse" as his chestnut locks fell in ringlets to the ground. With a desperate lunge he got to his feet. "You're going to pay for this. I'll tell my mother."

"What's going on out there?" A tall, stately young woman called from the side door of the big white frame house where the Remingtons lived in Canton, New York. She was dressed in the long, full skirt and high, pleated blouse that was the fashion in 1869. "You're making too much noise. What on earth . . .?"

She stopped abruptly. Her eight-year-old son, a sturdy tow-headed boy large for his age, was standing dazedly with a pair of scissors in his hand. A neighbor's boy stood glaring at him with tears in his eyes.

11

"Fred! What have you been up to? What are you doing with those shears?"

"We was playing Indian, Mother," her son explained.

"We *were* playing Indian," she corrected him automatically. She took a closer look at the neighbor's boy. "Junior, what's the matter with your hair?"

"It's nothing, Missus Remington." He ran his hand through his shorn locks in an effort to conceal the damage. "Fred was scalping me. I guess it was real funny."

She looked from one to the other. "I don't call it funny. Junior, you go on home. I'll be over to see your mother later. Fred, come inside. I'm going to have a talk with you."

"You shouldn't interfere, Mother. Women don't know nothing 'bout fighting," Fred muttered defiantly. Nevertheless he followed her into the house as his friend and victim made a quick getaway.

Taking him to the wide window seat, she made Fred sit down beside her. "Why must you always get in trouble?" she cried in exasperation. "If it isn't one thing, it's another. If your father had been here when you were younger, things would have been different. If it hadn't been for the war . . ."

The word "war" brought a picture to Fred's mind of his father in a splendid dark blue uniform gleaming with gold braid, riding up on a big white horse to his Grandfather Sackrider's home. Actually, he didn't remember his father's return from the Civil War, he had merely conjured it up later. The truth was his father had come to the house on foot, in duststained civilian clothes, his face gray with fatigue and lean from privation.

"When I grow up I'm going to be a soldier like Father," he said solemnly.

For punishment Fred was confined to his room with only a bowl of bread and milk for supper. He didn't mind too much, for only the day before he had sneaked out one of the books of a two-volume set from his father's library called *Manners, Customs, and Conditions of the North American Indians.* Now he opened it on his bed and, flopping himself down on all fours, turned through the pages. The text was much too difficult for him, and he ignored it completely. What he liked were the pictures, for the author, George Catlin, was also an artist, and the book was liberally illustrated with engravings of Indians and Western landscapes. The Indians had somewhat the aspect of wooden dolls and the landscapes were fuzzy, but Fred, at the age of eight, was not super-critical. The illustrations opened up to him a land of enchantment and danger—a land that was altogether unlike the safe and peaceful Canton village.

He put the book aside finally and went over to kneel in front of his window, resting his head on his hands, with his elbows on the sill. Outside, he could see the old nag belonging to their next-door neighbor, grazing placidly in the tiny pasture behind their house. She was a pitiful creature, with ribs showing plainly, lean flanks, and a hide that looked as if moths lived in it; but he liked watching her far better than his father's own sleek, plump mare. It was as though he could see through the scrawny nag, see why she held her head as she did and what muscles she used to raise her forelegs.

It struck him that horses were like people—all different. Some were fat and some were thin; some were nervous and full of little jerky movements and others were calm and strong, like the dapple gray down at the firehouse. The firehouse was the thing he liked best in Canton. He went down there nearly every day to talk with the men and to look over their horses. The men told him they had adopted him for their mascot. Just the day before, he had had his picture taken with them, wearing a fire hat just like theirs. They had promised him a print when the

13

picture was developed. He could hardly wait to show it to his father . . .

He heard the door slam downstairs and then the sound of his father's footsteps in the hall. With a quick dive he was on his bed again, pulling the light coverlet over him. Propped against the pillows, he was engrossed in making marks in a school notebook with a stubby pencil when his father entered his room a few minutes later.

Most businessmen in Canton came home for supper at six o'clock or so. Colonel Remington, who was editor of the Canton *Plain Dealer*, rarely arrived before eight or even later. This evening it was nearly nine, and the last rays of light from the late July sun were rapidly fading. His wife protested about the innumerable meetings that detained him far past mealtime.

"It isn't enough that you fought in the Civil War. Now you must fight another war for the Republicans," Fred often heard her say. He wasn't sure what Republicans were, except that they were his father's political party, so that meant they were good.

Colonel Seth Pierrepont Remington was a tall man, still young, with an impressive dark mustache and side whiskers. He walked with a military gait and had the air of one accustomed to command. Fred glowed with pride when they walked down the street together, and it seemed to him that everyone noticed what a wonderful father he had. By nature the Colonel was a man of fiery temperament, but as he approached his only son's bedside, his manner was gentle.

"I understand you got yourself in trouble, my boy."

"Yes, I guess so, Father." Fred tried to make his voice repentant—and failed.

"Tell me about it." The Colonel sat down on the edge of the bed.

"I was just playing."

14

"As I understand it, you went out for somebody's scalp. That's pretty serious playing."

"I didn't hurt him." Fred looked down and resumed the marks he was making in the notebook. "All I did was cut off his hair. He was an Indian chief and I was a general. I had to teach him a lesson."

"Listen, son." The Colonel put his hand on Fred's shoulder. "In the first place, it wouldn't have been the right thing to do even if you had been a real general. You see, scalping is an Indian custom, but to white men it is pretty barbarous. We should teach the Indians our way of life, not imitate their more brutal practices."

"Yes, Father," Fred said dutifully.

The crease of a frown appeared between his father's eyebrows. "You don't understand what I'm talking about. I hope you will someday. In the meantime I want you to promise me you won't do any more scalping."

"I promise." Fred would have promised his father anything.

"Well now, that's enough of a lecture for tonight." The Colonel rose. "I see you are doing your homework. That's good. Your mother would approve of that. What is it? Arithmetic? Writing?" He leaned over to pick up the notebook, which Fred reluctantly let slip out of his grasp. "Good grief," he exclaimed, his eyes fixed on the open page. "Is this the way you do your work?"

All along the margins were drawings—rough, childish, crude, but unmistakably of a horse, one horse, an old nag seen from different angles.

Fred said nothing, waiting for the expected scolding. It did not come.

"Amazing," muttered his father. "Altogether amazing. My son, I foresee your future. You are going to be a great artist."

Fred squirmed uneasily. Even he didn't think his scribblings were that good. "I don't want to be an artist," he said finally. "I want to be a soldier like you."

Canton, in Upper New York State, was a pleasant town to live in, with big, rambling frame houses, widely spaced and separated by grass lawns and high walls or low picket fences. Sidewalks, when there were any, were of wood. The cobblestone streets were lined with elms and at night were lit by gas lamps. They had been laid out in a random manner, and it was a matter of local pride that there were practically no cross intersections. Driving through town was somewhat like trying to find one's way through a labyrinth.

The longest street, though not the straightest, was Main Street, on which were the offices of Colonel Remington's *Plain Dealer* and also the haberdashery run by his brother William. At the edge of town was the recently founded St. Lawrence University, for which Fred's grandfather, Reverend Seth Remington, a Universalist minister, had raised the funds, thinking it would be only a theological school. There were not, as yet, very many students.

Fred had been born in his Grandfather Remington's house on October 1, 1861, just two months after his father had left to help James B. Swain organize the Eleventh New York Cavalry, known as "Scott's 900." The Reverend Remington had later fallen on hard times; he even had to borrow on the money he collected for the university. After a few months Fred's mother had taken the boy to live with her parents, the Deacon Sackriders. Colonel Remington hadn't returned to Canton until 1867, when the son he had never seen was nearly six years old, a chubby, healthy, pink-cheeked youngster, already slightly spoiled by the attention lavished on him by two sets of indulgent grandparents.

Though no Indians rode the streets of Canton echoing war

16

cries and brandishing tomahawks, it still had much to offer a growing boy—outside of scalping. In the winters, which were long and cold, there were tobogganing and other snow sports. In the summers the possibilities were endless.

The woods around the town were green and inviting, and Fred hiked through them daily, sometimes stopping to climb trees or hunt, sometimes going as far as Paradise Valley five miles away to visit a little boy named Addison Irving Bacheller, who lived on a farm with his parents.

On other days Fred fished or swam in the Grass River, just outside of town where the mouth of the Little River flowed into the Grass.

He was the best swimmer among the boys, but he was not supposed to go without his mother's consent.

"Mother, may I go swimming?" he asked her each time.

"It's much too cold. You'd better not this afternoon."

"No, Ma'am." He hoped she wouldn't notice that his hair was still wet from the dip he had taken *before* he made his request.

But he wouldn't go alone. He never liked to be alone. When swimming was on his schedule, he would go from one end of Main Street to the other, rounding up his companions. It was taken for granted that Fred was their leader, but one day a young boy named Donald protested that he wasn't in the mood for swimming.

"Come along anyway," Fred suggested.

"Oh, all right."

When they reached the river bank, Fred once more insisted that Donald go in the water. "I'll race you to the opposite shore."

"I don't feel like it," Donald said stubbornly.

"Then I'll make you."

Fred started after him with his fists. When he was around the firehouse the men there taught him the rudiments of boxing. He was good at it, and his friends knew they didn't have a chance against him.

"You win," Don said.

He stripped and plunged into the water, Fred after him. Don headed for the opposite shore, toward a path where some young ladies from the university were taking a walk.

"Not that way," Fred called desperately. "There are some women over there."

"Give up?" Don called back, laughing and splashing.

"I give up." Fred turned around and headed back.

Don had an easy victory that time. Fred purposely avoided women because he felt so awkward, tongue-tied, oversized in their presence. The only ones who didn't make him turn and run were very little girls, and these he teased mercilessly—for instance the neighbor's child, whose dog he once painted a bright green. That had brought him a scolding from his mother too.

His father had given him a stern talking-to as well, but he had broken down in the middle of it and chuckled. "Well, I guess that's the first live animal you ever painted," he remarked.

It was also the last painting Fred did for quite some time, but he did plenty of drawing, with crayons or just a stubby pencil—in school when he was supposed to be listening to the teacher; on brown wrapping paper at a friendly grocer's; in his Grandfather Sackrider's house. His sketches were almost always of horses, Indians, and soldiers.

When Fred was thirteen, his father was offered the political position of Collector of Ports, at Ogdensburg, New York, directly across the border from Canada, eighteen miles from Canton. After selling the *Plain Dealer*, the family moved up there, where Fred swam in the Saint Lawrence instead of the Grass, and made new friends at the Ogdensburg school, particularly a boy of his own age named John Howard.

He still talked about being a soldier when he grew up, and a year after they moved to Ogdensburg his father agreed to send Fred to a military academy in Burlington, Vermont. He liked it well enough. The drilling wasn't too hard; there was fine swimming; and occasionally there were special excursions to Fort Ticonderoga and other points of historical interest. But he stayed only one year, because his family learned that some of the boys at the academy drank and smoked and they decided it wasn't the right place for him.

"I swear I'll never take a drink," Fred told John Howard afterward.

That summer he spent most of his time in Canton, staying with his Grandfather and Grandmother Sackrider. The house was soon noisy and overflowing with his former schoolmates, and the Deacon, who liked his peace and quiet, protested, "Don't you have a home of your own?"

"You know you're glad to have me," Fred said mischievously.

He bought oil paints and a smock and turned the Sackrider barn into a studio for himself, paying small boys a nickel to hold the Deacon's horse still while he drew it. At Burlington he had become interested in ancient history, and the first painting he did, out in the barn, was of a Gaul chained to a post in a dungeon with a Roman sentinel standing guard. It was far from a great painting, or even a very good one, but there was a certain vigor to it that caused his Uncle Robert Sackrider to exclaim, "Stick to it, boy. You'll be an artist yet."

But his grandmother found the subject matter unpleasant, and the painting, done on board, remained out in the barn.

He also did a portrait of his Grandfather Sackrider. "I like to draw you because your face is rough and full of wrinkles," he explained, not too flatteringly. The portrait stayed out in the barn too.

19

The next year, in 1876, Fred was enrolled in the Highland Military Academy in Worcester, Massachusetts. At fifteen, he already weighed a hundred and eighty pounds and was five feet eight inches tall, blond and blue-eyed as a Viking, a man except for his chubby, boyish face. The academy tailor fitted him with a uniform and his new schoolmates dubbed him "Bud." Discipline was strict and he spent several hours a day at military drill and trying to master military science from Upton's *Infantry Tactics*.

He didn't like the new school and ran away. Of course he was caught and brought back, and was confined to his room for three days. He resigned himself to staying, devoting most of his time to athletics, which he liked. His school marks were just passing, although he discovered he didn't mind English composition.

Another student, named Julian Wilder, caught him making a picture of American troopers fighting Indians.

"I have a friend who draws better than you do," Julian commented after a critical study of Fred's handiwork.

"Who's that?"

"Scott Turner. He lives in Augusta, Maine, and he writes to me." He drew a letter from his pocket. "Here, I'll show you." The letter was amply illustrated with sketches of one sort and another.

"You're right," Fred acknowledged after a hasty survey. "He's a heck of a better artist than I." He hesitated. "Do you suppose he'd write to me?"

The correspondence that developed between Fred and the Maine artist was the most interesting thing that happened to him at Highland. In his first letter he confessed, "I admire your mode of shading which I cannot get the hang of." This was his first attempt to "talk shop" with another artist.

Scott answered promptly with a letter full of sketches. Fred was delighted. Since Scott asked for it, he sent a photograph of himself, though he was embarrassed: "You can burn it but don't throw it into the back yard or it may scare some wandering hen to death." He confided to his new friend that he had never drawn a woman—except once and then had washed her out—or a ship, and he begged for a battle between "Russians and Turks or Indians."

In one letter Scott included some sketches of men and women in evening dress. Fred was indignant. "Don't send me any more women or dudes," he wrote.

He and Julian Wilder, who had introduced him to the Maine artist, become close friends. They exchanged confidences and got into all kinds of scrapes together. Once they sneaked into the armory and carried on a mock duel in which Fred used a saber and Julian brandished an old rusty musket. Another time they had a wrestling match, and Julian came out of it with a broken collarbone and a dislocated arm.

"You may be an artist but you're no sissy," he commented ruefully.

By the time Fred left Highland he had decided that he no longer wanted to be a soldier. He still admired them but he knew he could never be happy obeying commands and submitting to discipline. He was just too much of an individualist and confessed as much to his father when he returned home to Ogdensburg.

"I'm not surprised," the Colonel said. "I've wanted to get into your head for a long time that warfare wasn't all banners and glory. There's a new art school at Yale and I'm arranging for you to go there. We'll see if this talent of yours amounts to anything."

"Does Mother know about it?" Fred asked.

"We'll tell her."

21

"Yale is not a bad idea," his mother said when she heard about it. "But I think Fred should take some business courses. He'll never make a living by painting pictures."

"Well, maybe he can study both art and business," Colonel Remington compromised.

CHAPTER · 2

"Our subject today is a masterpiece of Greek sculpture," Professor Niemeyer, a melancholy, bearded man, addressed the only two students of his Yale art class on the first day. "The original is in Rome. We have here a plaster model. It is the immortal Faun of Praxiteles. You will note the beauty and grace of the male form. Is it any wonder that Mr. Nathaniel Hawthorne should have used it as a symbol for the sublime in his fine novel, *The Marble Faun*?"

As the good professor droned on in his stiff, German-accented English, Fred moved restlessly in his chair, crossing and uncrossing his long legs. He had come to Yale because it was his father's wish, though he didn't mind learning more about drawing techniques. But what did he care about the Faun of Prax— whatever his name was. His eyes rested hostilely on the subject of the professor's lecture and the other busts of classic art that lined the walls of the basement classroom in the year of 1878.

Didn't those old boys ever take a look at real people? he asked himself. They made everyone look exactly alike, all with the same regular features, the same blank expression. Surely there had been some gross and crafty Greeks, little wizened ones or old wrinkled ones, the sort it would be fun to draw. Anything would be better than this "faun" who looked as though he'd never been in a prizefight in his life.

"I shall leave you now to let you feast your eyes on this statue's perfection," the professor said. "When the full appreciation of it reaches you, then and only then should you make sketches. It may not happen today, but if it does, crayons and drawing paper are in the cupboard. Good afternoon, gentlemen."

"Are you feasting your eyes, chum?" The voice of Fred's classmate broke the silence that followed the professor's departure.

Fred looked over in surprise. He had given his fellow classmate only a cursory glance when the lecture had started—and had judged him to be just another upper classman with the usual disdain of freshmen. Now he saw a heavily tanned young man, of slighter build than his own, with humorous eyes beneath rather shaggy eyebrows.

"To be honest, I was almost asleep," Fred said with a yawn. "Is it against the rules to have fresh air in an art room?"

"Not only against the rules, it's rank heresy," the other informed him mockingly. "A breeze might disturb the sacred dust that has been accumulating through the ages." He got up and took the seat next to Fred. "My name's Poultney Bigelow. "What's yours?"

"Remington. Fred."

The name Remington meant something in Canton and Ogdensburg, but no one in Yale had heard of either the *Plain Dealer* or the Colonel's Civil War record, and Poultney made no comment except to nod.

"Well, Fred, it looks as though we are to be fellow prisoners. We might as well make the most of it. My friends call be 'Big,' which is inappropriate but less of a mouthful than Poultney. Your first year here?"

23

"That's right and I'm hoping it will be my last." Fred laughed shortly.

"You don't think much of the Faun of Praxiteles?" Big regarded him with a quizzical expression.

"No."

"Just to satisfy my curiosity—why not?"

Fred got up and stood in front of the offending statue, his hands in his pockets. "Take a good look. A grown man, leaning against a tree stump like a girl waiting for her beau. Note the pointed ears. Nobody has ears like that. And why does he have to drape a lionskin around his shoulders? I'll bet my last nickel he never shot it."

"Maybe he was cold," Big commented.

"Cold or not, he looks foolish," Fred burst out. He sat down in his chair with a sigh. "Shouldn't we look like we're studying or something in case the professor comes back?"

"You needn't worry about that," Big assured him. "Professor Niemeyer feels he's done his duty by us for today. He's off somewhere doing his own painting."

"What does he paint?" Fred asked suspiciously.

"He's a devotee of the French classicists," Big explained. "His painting, 'Gutenberg Inventing Movable Type,' was hung in the French Salon."

Fred did not know who the French classicists were nor what it meant to be hung in the French Salon, but he sensed the professor's art was not for him. "Why should anyone want to paint Gutenberg?" he asked. "He's been dead for centuries."

Big laughed. "You have a point there. You're a rebel, aren't you, Fred?"

Fred gave him a puzzled look. "Heck, no. I'm a Yankee."

"I didn't mean a Southern Rebel. I mean you don't let other people make up your mind for you."

"Oh that! I guess you're right." Idly he began to sketch on a

24

scrap of paper. "I don't give a hoot for all this stuff you find in the museums. But I do like to draw—horses and soldiers and such."

"There's some 'stuff' in museums that shows soldiers and horses. I suppose you know Detaille and de Neuville?"

"Never heard of them," Fred admitted.

"They've been doing some pretty good things on the Franco-Prussian War. Maybe there are some examples here." Big walked over to the shelves where the art books and portfolios were kept. "Ah, here we are," he said after a moment's search.

For the rest of the afternoon Fred reveled in the studies done by the two French contemporary painters, Alphonse Marie de Neuville and Jean Baptist Edouard Detaille, names he would never be able to pronounce with Big's excellent French accent. The insolent Prussian officers, shrewd French peasants, common soldiers, and above all the horses, delighted and excited him.

After Professor Niemeyer returned to dismiss the session, the two young men crossed the shaded campus together. Fred learned that his new friend had no serious ambitions to be an artist, though he had studied perspective in Europe. He was much more interested in writing. As a boy, he had gone to school in France and later, in Germany, where Prince Wilhelm, the future Kaiser, had been a playmate. When presented with a bow and a quiver of arrows, the young Prince had been thrilled and had insisted that he and Big play Indians. Listening to all this, Fred found it quite interesting but felt rather sorry for Big because he had missed the pleasures of an American boyhood.

That evening a wide-eyed freshman who shared his dormitory collared him. "I saw you walking across the campus with Poultney Bigelow," he said. "You don't waste much time getting acquainted with the top men here, do you?"

"How do you mean?" Fred asked.

"Why, he's the editor of the *Yale Courant* and probably the most popular man at Yale. You know—his father, John Bigelow, was Ambassador to France and Germany and I don't know what-all. He's enormously wealthy."

"What has that got to do with me?" Fred asked angrily. He liked Big, no matter who his father was.

In a few weeks Fred settled down to life at Yale. While the business courses held his interest no more than did the art class, he found a release for his energies in boxing and football practice. Anyone, even a freshman, could go in for football practice, but playing on the team was another matter. Fred looked on with envy when the Varsity left for Boston to fight Harvard in late November. The news that Yale had won—one to zero—reached the students' ears before the return of the heroes, and everyone went wild. By special dispensation, the dean dismissed classes that day to let the students meet the victorious team. They were there at the depot, three hundred strong, shouting and yelling.

As the men got off the train and were lifted onto the shoulders of their proud classmates, Fred turned to Big, who had come with him. "Gee, what wouldn't I give to be one of them."

"I wouldn't. For my money, football is a messy, scroungy sort of sport. Give me boat racing any time."

The two young men had other differences. Big was an excellent scholar, and his grades were as consistently high as Fred's were mediocre. Fred tolerated this, but he steadfastly refused to accompany Big to the Sunday teas at the home of John Weir, head of the art school, who was a family friend of the Bigelows.

"You're missing something," Big told him with a touch of irony. "Last Sunday we compared Greek and Gothic architecture and the origins of each."

"I guess I'll just have to manage to exist without it," commented Fred, who had no more interest in Greek and Gothic architecture than in the Faun of Praxiteles.

In spite of the dissimilarities of their tastes in sports, in culture, and in practically everything else, a close friendship developed between them, a friendship that gave Fred the feeling that his first year at Yale was not altogether completely wasted. Nevertheless he was genuinely glad when vacation came.

It was a fine summer, during which Fred alternated between boating on the Saint Lawrence while he was in Ogdensburg with his parents, painting in his Grandfather Sackrider's barn while he was in Canton, and hiking on various excursions to Cranberry Lake in the Adirondacks, where he could fish and hunt small game.

"It's time you decided what you want to do with your life," his mother advised him.

"I want to enjoy it," he told her. "I want to spend as much time as I can doing the things I like to do."

"Be serious, son," she said. "You'll never make a living fishing or swimming, any more than you will drawing pictures."

"Leave the boy alone," the Colonel cautioned. "He'll find out where he's going soon enough."

"All I'm doing is trying to make him think of the future," Mrs. Remington insisted. "One of these days he'll be married with a wife to support. How is he going to manage?"

"Married?" Fred snorted. "That will be the day." Although he was nineteen and a tall, strapping youth on whom young women often looked approvingly, he had neved dated girls, and still avoided conversation with them whenever he could.

He took off for Canton again soon after this conversation, arriving in time for a county fair. The fair was always a gala occasion. Farmers displayed their prize pigs and cattle; their wives entered preserves and cakes in contests; children rode the carousels and the swings. The townspeople, young and old, wandered around viewing the various exhibits, exchanging news, and trying their luck at the games.

Fred went for one reason only: to watch the horse racing. It didn't matter which horses won, he simply loved to watch them run. Making sure a sketch pad was in his pocket, he arrived early and took a place on a front bench. He was so absorbed that he didn't notice the people around him until he heard a voice at his side. "Fred Remington! What are you doing in town?"

He looked up to see his old friend from Paradise Valley, Addison Irving Bacheller, now a grown man with bushy yellow hair, grinning down at him.

He jumped up and offered his hand. "Good to see you, Ad. Have a seat."

"Sure. I have a couple of friends I'd like you to meet."

Fred noticed then that two people stood beside Bacheller—a man of his own age and a young woman.

"This is Will Caten and his sister, Miss Eva Caten," Ad said. "They're going to St. Lawrence next month and are down here looking us over. As a man who has already finished his freshman year, I have the honor of showing them around." He turned to his companions. "Fred Remington is the best swimmer and the best football player ever to come out of Canton."

"Glad to meet you," Fred managed to stammer. He shook hands with Will Caten and his sister.

Eva Caten's hands were small and white, and she was tiny, barely reaching to his shoulder. He was vaguely aware of the deep blue of her eyes, which seemed to reflect the blue stones in the brooch at her throat.

"I'm pleased to know you, Mr. Remington." Her voice was soft, calm and clear.

To Fred's discomfiture, Ad Bacheller decided that Eva should sit between the two of them, but much to his relief she didn't try to talk. When the races began, he forgot her completely and, drawing out his pad, began to sketch.

"I like the way you draw, Mr. Remington," Eva said suddenly. "You seem to make the horses move, even though they are on paper."

"That's what I'm trying to do," he said abruptly. "Anyone can draw horses standing still."

"Not anyone." She gave him a roguish smile. "If I drew a horse, no one would know whether it was a tree or a house."

Her way of speaking made him laugh, and to his astonishment he no longer minded her being there.

"Is this your first visit to Canton, Miss Caten?"

"Yes. It's a lovely place, so much less commercial than Gloversville. And the people are nice too, hospitable and friendly. I'm glad I'm going to be living here."

"I am too," Fred said.

After the fair he walked with her to the friends' house where she was staying. He called on her the next day and the next, and every day for the length of her visit. They went for buggy rides, took walks along the shaded streets of the town or out into the country along the river. Not only was Eva beautiful, Fred admitted to himself; she made him feel at ease. Before she left he knew that he had fallen in love. Everyone else in Canton knew it too.

When she returned to Gloversville, he made trips there to see her, met her parents, her two sisters, Clara and Emma, and her other brother, Fred. They were a friendly family and he liked them immensely. It didn't bother him that Mr. Caten, an official of the Fondo, Johnstown and Gloversville Railroad, was better off than his own father, and that the household had a standard of living considerably higher than he had known. In fact, it seemed right that Eva, or Missie as her family called her, should have been born to luxury.

He hated to go back to Yale. The thought of art classes for another year was intolerable. But he couldn't disappoint his father. He wrote Eva regularly when he got back, confident that she would be interested in everything that happened to him. There was a lot to tell her.

Big, who was still editor of the *Courant*, had a brainstorm and decided the magazine should be illustrated. Fred was added to the staff as art editor. His first published picture appeared in the issue of November 2, 1879. It was entitled "College Riff-raff" and showed a student football player, battered and bandaged. When Professor Niemeyer saw it, he was outraged.

"All the time you have been here, you learn nothing," he stormed. "The picture, it is not art. It is terrible."

Fred agreed with him. The rival campus weekly, the *Yale Record*, was also indignant at what the editors called a lowering of literary standards to please popular taste. But the circulation of the *Courant* increased, and the paper was able to declare a dividend.

The student football player of the cartoon bore a certain resemblance to Fred himself. Football was still his favorite sport, and this year he was on the Yale team, captained by a mustached young man named Walter Camp, who had already made a reputation for himself by championing scrimmage, based on English rugby, in preference to "scrummage," which had been used before. At Thanksgiving, Fred played in the Yale-Princeton game, and even won a press notice as an outstanding young forward.

But with his new dream of getting married, which he hadn't yet mentioned to Eva, he still felt that he was wasting his time.

"What's the use of memorizing a lesson for one day which you forget the next?" he demanded of Big.

"No use," his friend agreed cheerfully. "The system here is all wrong. Learning should be not a question of memorizing but of assimilating knowledge until it is part of you. We're kept so busy on our lessons that we never have time to think." He launched into a discussion of the difference between American and European universities.

Fred didn't even try to follow him. "If my father wasn't set on my staying here, I'd walk out tomorrow. Now I'm afraid I'll have to stick it out the entire four years."

He was wrong. When he went home for the Christmas holidays, he found his father in very poor health, and postponed his return to Yale to be with him. A few weeks later, on February 10, 1880, Colonel Remington died of a cerebral hemorrhage.

Although Fred had been separated from his father much of his life, he had always felt close to him. It seemed unbelievable that he was no longer there to give approval or disapproval to whatever his son might do.

"I'm not going back to Yale," he announced to his mother shortly after the funeral. "I'm through being a schoolboy."

Mrs. Remington did not argue with him. "There's something I should tell you, Frederic. Your father left you a small inheritance. It rather worries me. I know how reckless you can be. I want you to promise me not to touch it until you're ready to settle down in a home of your own."

To mention money so soon after his father's death seemed a sacrilege to Fred, and he said so.

"Well, maybe you should go to work," she sighed. "That should teach you what money means."

He obliged her by accepting a position as a clerk in an Ogdensburg store, but he stuck it out for only a few days. He tried several other jobs in the course of the next few months, but they were all equally distasteful to him. He wasn't sure what he was cut out to do, but he knew it wasn't sitting at a desk all day. His mother persuaded him to see an old political friend of his father, who arranged for him to work as a clerk in the governor's office in Albany. This didn't appeal to him either, but it seemed a good idea to get away from home for a while. The house on Hamilton Street was a gloomy place without his father, and his mother encouraged him to accept the job, since "being in politics," as she referred to his lowly position, to her meant a brilliant future.

The Albany job was as dreary as he had feared, and he fled to Gloversville his first free week end. He hadn't seen Missie since his father's death. She wore a dress of deep-pink striped silk, with a fashionable bustle, and to Fred she gave the impression of being made of porcelain, as fragile and pretty as a Dresden doll. But he was unable to tell her so, having no gift for phrasing compliments.

At supper Mr. Caten offered Fred his sympathy for his recent bereavement.

"I suppose you're going to take over the Saint Lawrence *Journal* now?" he asked. This was an Ogdensburg newspaper in which Colonel Remington had bought part interest shortly after they had moved there.

Fred shook his head. "Father sold his interest before he died. Even if he hadn't, I don't feel I'm cut out to be a newspaperman."

"Eva tells me you're working for the governor," Mr. Caten went on. "What sort of man is he?"

"I never see him. He's not even aware I exist," Fred said truthfully. It didn't occur to him that he should try to make his work sound more important in the eyes of Missie's father.

After supper he and Missie went out and sat on the porch swing. The night air was warm and caressing, fragrant with the perfumes of the late summer flowers. For the first time in many months Fred felt content.

"It's good to see you again, Miss Caten," he broke the silence. "I've missed you."

"I've missed you too, Mr. Remington," she said softly.

He reached over and took her hand. She did not draw it away. "There's something I've been meaning to ask you for a long time," he burst out.

"Yes?" her voice encouraged him.

"I mean," he stammered, "I mean I've known for a long time that I want to marry you. I love you and if you won't marry me, I won't ever marry anybody. Will you, Miss Caten?"

It wasn't a very elegant proposal but Eva didn't seem to notice. "I love you too," she said quietly. "Of course we'll have to ask Father. He may think we're too young to get married."

Fred felt his spirits soaring somewhere out beyond the stars. "I'm almost twenty. That's not young. Your father can't refuse."

Writing a letter to a man asking for his daughter's hand is not an easy matter. Fred spent hours laboring over it, and then, because he didn't think his own handwriting was impressive enough, he persuaded one of his colleagues in the office to copy it for him. They borrowed a sheet of engraved stationery with *Executive Chambers, Albany* at the top of it. The letter, dated August 25, 1880, read:

> Mr. Lawton Caten, Dear Sir, I pen these lines to you on a most delicate subject and hope they will at least receive your consideration. For a year I have known your daughter, Eva, and during that time have contracted a deep affection for her . . . I feel warranted now in asking whether or not you will consent to an engagement between us . . . Hoping this will not be distasteful, allow me to sign. Your Obedient Servant.

"This ought to do it," Fred's colleague commented as, with a flourish, he signed *Fred'c Remington.*

"I hope so," Fred said fervently.

He waited impatiently for a week and then the answer, marked *Personal*, arrived at his office. Mr. Caten liked him very much, the letter said. He had nothing against him. However, he didn't feel that Fred's employment record indicated the stable qualities that he would prefer in a husband for his daughter. It had been a hard decision to make, but he had five children. He had to do what was right for them.

That evening Fred found a tearful note from Missie waiting for him at his boardinghouse. Her father's decision had grieved her very much, she said. There was nothing either of them could do about it, of course, and it would be better if they didn't see each other any more. At the end of the letter she had written "perhaps, sometime" but then she had apparently changed her mind and crossed these two words out. The note was signed simply, *Always your friend, Eva Caten.*

The words "perhaps, sometime" softened the blow and gave Fred some hope. He had a healthy ego and was sure Missie cared for him. He spent all night writing her letters and finally tore up all but one, which he mailed. She didn't answer. Nor did she reply to his subsequent letters. There finally came a moment when he was forced to admit, with deep hurt, that Missie was lost to him.

It was a dreary, lonely winter. He held five or six jobs in Albany for brief periods and hated them all equally. He disliked the town, the streets, the bustle, the people. He brooded a great deal, kept to himself, lost weight, and finally fell sick.

"There's nothing seriously wrong with you," the doctor told him. "What you need is a change of air. Why don't you take a trip?"

"What for? Where would I go?" Fred asked apathetically.

"What interests you most?"

34

"The outdoors. Trees and mountains and lakes. Any place that's not cluttered up with office buildings."

"Why not go out West?" the doctor suggested.

CHAPTER · *3*

On August 20, 1881, a year after Fred was refused permission to marry Missie, he was on a train headed West, his destination the great Territory of Montana. The journey as far as Chicago was not completely new to him, for his mother had taken him when he was a child to visit relatives in Burlington, Illinois. But when he boarded the train bound for Minnesota, he knew he was really leaving the familiar world behind—the pretty New England towns and green landscapes. When he changed to the Northern Pacific Railroad at St. Paul and set off across the Northern forests and the Dakota Badlands, he was beside himself with excitement.

It was a great disappointment the first half of the three-hundred-mile stretch from Bismarck to Miles City was hidden by night. For a long time Fred lay awake on his couch in the sleeping car—a luxury he had allowed himself with the first of his father's inheritance—listening to the rhythmic clank of the wheels and visualizing the savage land through which the train was rushing like the wind. He was up at dawn, watching the red streaks of the sunrise from the rear platform. The wheat fields and farms that the daylight revealed came as a surprise. Near the railroad at least, civilization had already stretched its tentacles. The train stopped at a way station on the banks of the Little Missouri, where the passengers piled out to a breakfast of flapjacks and thick slices of bacon and steaming coffee. Then they were off again past Sentinel Butte, and soon the conductor, who had been keeping a paternal eye on Fred, informed him they had crossed the Dakota boundaries and were now in Montana.

"That's great!" Fred exclaimed, staring out the window at the rolling plains. "Where are the buffalo herds?"

The conductor, a wiry man with black handle-bar mustaches, laughed. "You'll find them all right if you keep going, kid, but not as many as a few years back. If you ask me, it's a crime the way folks shoot them down for the hides, leaving the carcasses to rot in the sun."

Fred agreed with him. The West, without herds of wandering buffalo, was inconceivable. Those who might aid and abet such a situation were no less than criminals.

The conductor looked at him curiously. "Meeting your folks out here?"

"Nope," Fred said shortly. The implication that he was a child who needed looking after irked him. After all, he was nearly twenty, and a man.

"On your own, eh?" persisted the man. "Got a job with the railway? Or going to stake a claim or homestead a cattle ranch?"

"Something like that." He was not going to confess that he was traveling for his health and that his mother had extracted his solemn promise to return within two months.

At five that afternoon the train stopped at Miles City on the mouth of the Tongue, which was, at that time, the end of the Northern Pacific line. Since preparations were being made to carry the railroad on to Billings, the town was full of graders, tie-men, track-layers, and other railroad workers waiting for orders.

As Fred knew, Miles City had been named for General Nelson A. Miles, already a legendary figure, the Civil War veteran whose troops had defeated Crazy Horse and Lame Deer and who had later captured Chief Joseph of the Nez Percés. Miles had arrived in that vicinity five years before, in August of 1876, to carry on where Custer had left off. It took Fred only a few minutes to walk over to the log buildings of Fort Keogh, where Miles had had his headquarters. But the soldiers on duty informed him Miles had pulled out the previous year. There was no need of him now that Indians were no longer a threat in this part of the country.

Fred was sorry not to see the famous general in person, but consoled himself on his way back by stopping in the general store and purchasing some heavy brown ducking trousers and jacket, a pair of high-top boots, and a wide-brimmed sombrero. He changed behind a pile of packing boxes and rolled his city suit into a small bundle, feeling less conspicuous when he resumed his walk, though the newness of the outfit bothered him. Surreptitiously he leaned over, swooped up a handful of mud from the dirt road, and wiped it over the sides of his trousers.

He slept in the Saint Cloud Hotel that night and the next morning bought a stagecoach ticket to Billings. His fellow passengers included a couple of prospectors, an elderly man who was buying a cattle ranch, and a young woman who was joining her fiancé on a farm he was homesteading. Women seemed out of place in this country. Fred never noticed whether she was pretty or not, for he sat as far away from her as he could, his eyes fixed on the prairies.

The rumor had spread that Billings was soon to have a railroad; the town was crowded with a motley population, with people camping in tents for lack of proper housing. With some difficulty Fred found a room in a boardinghouse. Before noon the next day he had completed the purchase of a spotted pony and a saddle from a Crow Indian (dressed not in feathered bonnet and war paint but rather pathetically in old army trousers and a shawl over his shoulders). Fred then rode away from the crowded metropolis and across the plains to the one place he felt he must see—the site of the battlefield where on June 25, 1876, General Custer and five troops of the Seventh United States Cavalry had lost their lives.

In six years' time the battlefield had already become a place of pilgrimage, wooden crosses marking the graves of those who had died there. Following the directions of the man at the nearby Crow Agency, Fred pulled up his horse on the hill where the massacre had taken place. The rays of the late-afternoon sun cast a misty light over the Little Big Horn, along which the Cheyennes and the Sioux had had their camps on that fatal day. How peaceful it all seemed now—the green, rolling hills and the little river meandering between willow bushes. I'm six years too late, Fred thought regretfully.

Impulsively he slid off his pony, letting her reins drag so she would not run away, propped himself against a rock, and began to draw a picture of Custer's last stand, using a stubby pencil and the sketch pad he had brought from the East. He realized it was a rough piece of work; he didn't even know for sure what kind of uniforms the men wore or how the Indians were dressed. Of Custer he remembered only that he had long yellow hair. He didn't learn till later that Custer had clipped his locks short before this battle. But with all its failings, the drawing had vigor and feeling.

"Someday, when I'm older and wiser, I'll do it as it should be done," Fred murmured to himself. He tucked the sketch pad back into his saddlebag, swung up on his pony, and headed back.

It was too late to reach Billings that night. He stopped off at an army cantonment in charge of a Major Bell, who in the custom of the times offered him shelter. Until very late he played cards with the soldiers, for whom the arrival of the Easterner was a diversion. Fred on his part was fascinated by their rough

38

talk and easy manners. Before the evening was over he had the beginning of a new vocabulary that would eventually come more natural to him than English as it was spoken at Yale.

The next day found him back at Billings, but only long enough to rescue his bag from the boardinghouse, dispose of his pony, and make the purchase of a repeating rifle and a brace of pistols. Then he took a stagecoach to Bozeman, talking the driver into letting him sit up beside him on top. With his sombrero on the back of his head and the security of the pistols on his belt, he felt himself a real Westerner for the first time.

"What are the chances of a holdup?" he asked the driver casually.

There had not been any recently, the driver assured him, though a year or so before, the roads were peppered with stage robbers who would as soon kill a stagecoach driver as eat their own breakfast. Fred felt as he had at Custer's battlefield—that he had arrived too late.

The road led them along the picturesque Yellowstone River, then cut across into the mountains. In the brilliant late summer sunlight the contrast of colors struck the artist in Fred like a vibrant chord. In place of the soft, varied greens of the East, here was a startling symphony, in which the vivid blue of the sky was a background for the red and gray and orange shadows of the jutting crags and the deep green of the pines.

At noon they stopped at a ranch where they were fed a mighty meal of mountain trout and roast fowl; then they proceeded along a fertile valley to a narrow gorge where a single misstep of their sure-footed steeds would have plunged them hundreds of feet into an abyss. The sun went down in a red holocaust behind snow-covered peaks and the moon came out, turning the river beneath them to a sea of jewels. Breathing deep the cold, invigorating mountain air, Fred forgot the cramped discomforts of hours in the driver's box. This was his country; he had come home.

At Bozeman, a frontier town dominated by saloons, Fred bought a sturdy gray mare and a saddle blanket and set off in the general direction of Helena, following a rutted wagon trail across rolling hills. Toward dusk he caught sight of a spiral of smoke in the distance. As he approached he saw an old man in shabby clothes cooking his dinner over an open fire at the side of a freighter's wagon—the sort that hauled goods from town to ranch.

"Howdy!" Fred called, reining in his mare.

"Howdy." The old man returned the greeting impassively.

"Say, could you tell me how far it is to town?"

"Up the road a piece. If you keep going you'll get there."

He did not say when he'd get there, and Fred lingered, hating to leave the inviting warmth of the fire and human companionship. "Pretty cold night, isn't it?"

The wagon freighter didn't deign to reply. "If you want some grub, come help yourself."

"Well, thanks." Fred slid off the mare promptly. "I sure am hungry."

He was, and the stale bacon and beans the old man served him on a battered tin plate tasted fine, as did the muddy brew of coffee that followed.

They ate in silence while the late twilight deepened into night and the hills turned black against the starry sky. In the distance an eerie howl startled the stillness.

"Wolves?" Fred asked.

"Nope. Coyotes."

The old man lit his pipe. Then, without any urging, he began to talk. Of his childhood in western New York. Of how as a young man—about Fred's age but skinnier—he had kicked up the traces and come West—the West of that long-ago being

40

Iowa. Year after year he had followed the receding frontiers, working as farmhand, cow puncher, logger, rider with wagon trains, taking whatever job the time and place offered.

"I've seen a-plenty, boy," he concluded. "But what I see now I don't like a dang bit."

"What do you mean?" Fred asked as he idly drew the old man's profile with a twig on the sandy soil.

"There ain't no West no more," he sputtered. "Any moment now the railroad will come along the Yellowstone, and a poor man like myself won't be able to make a living.

Fred remarked that there would be a need for men to tote supplies, even after the railroad came.

His comment only deepened the wagon freighter's pessimism. It was clear that he was not afraid of losing his job so much as he was afraid of the East catching up to him. Remembering how he had felt in crowded Miles City and even in Billings, Fred sympathized with him.

As the old man rambled on, a series of pictures formed in Fred's mind. He saw the silent, rolling hills around them invaded by a horde of men in derby hats, and gossiping women. He saw factories with smoking chimneys and the ever-more frequent rush and roar of trains. The worst was that this change was inevitable. The West as it had been was about to vanish forever. The more he thought about it, the bigger this "forever" loomed.

They slept in their blankets on the ground that night. It rained, not much but enough to wet them through. Before daylight the old man, in his faded cotton shirt and patched trousers, was out hunting his horse in the bleak, chilly hills. Fred built the fire while he was gone. After they had more coffee, Fred thanked him and rode off.

The old man's words, "There ain't no West no more," echoed in his ears, ungrammatically and unrelentingly. By worldly

41

standards the wagon freighter's life was a wretched one; after a lifetime of hard work he had barely enough to mend his harness and buy grease for his dilapidated wagon. He had no home, no family. But he had a freedom men at desks never know and he asked only that things remain as they were. In asking that he was asking the impossible. Waves of immigrants were on their way. Fred had seen them. New towns would spring up where there had once been only mountains and plains. Wild meadowland would be cultivated for corn and wheat and potatoes. The Indians would go as the buffalo had almost gone. Banks would stand where traders' shacks had once been . . .

Suddenly Fred knew what he wanted to do, knew it with the clarity of a lightning flash illuminating a dark countryside. He must, by means of charcoal and paints and pen and ink, make a permanent record of the country that Lewis and Clark had seen in its primeval state and which in subsequent decades had become a land of prospectors and traders and trappers that captured the imagination of people everywhere. The moment of this decision marked a turning point in his life.

He rode on to Helena, the new capital of the Montana Territory, where he found rich prospectors living in ornate mansions, riding around in carriages driven by coachmen in top hats and swallow-tailed coats. He left quickly, riding northward up through the solemn beauty of the Rockies, carrying his own bacon and beans and frying pan, not wanting to depend on the good will of infrequent travelers and the still more infrequent outpost towns.

He fished for trout in mountain streams and lakes and shot small game to supplement his diet, and learned to accept with equanimity the appearance of a great moose or the sight of white-tailed deer grazing in a pasture. His Miles City clothes became caked with mud and dust. He stopped shaving and though his beard was nothing to brag about, it covered the boyish contours of his face sufficiently to stop strangers from addressing him as "kid" or "young 'un." His blond hair grew almost as long as Custer's.

As the days passed, the resolution he had made after the night with the wagon freighter grew stronger. Whenever he stopped to eat or sleep or rest his horse, he made sketches—of the men he met, of his horse, of everything connected with Western life. When he ran out of sketch pads, he used whatever scraps of paper he could scavenge.

Along the Bow River one day he came upon a camp of Blackfeet in their native dress. At what seemed a safe distance he pulled up his horse and, still in his saddle, started sketching them. He looked up to see one of them raising his tomahawk menacingly in his direction. Fred spurred the mare and was off, not waiting to investigate. A mile further on, it struck him that for the first time in his life he had been in actual physical danger. The thought made him shiver; it also brought a curious exhilaration.

A couple of days later he awoke to find that his horse had disappeared. He suspected that the Blackfeet had followed him and made off with her, and wondered why they had left him with his scalp.

Horses were cheap in that country. He hiked over twenty miles of mountain country and at the next trading post bought himself a new one, a rambunctious little creature who didn't take to him at all. No sooner had he mounted than he was on the ground, much to the amusement of the men lounging around the trader's porch. It was the first time he was thrown, but it wouldn't be the last. His dignity suffered considerably.

He subdued the pony sufficiently so that she took him on up past the Canadian border, where he saw his first Mounted Police —bringing in a Blackfoot suspected of murder. He transferred the scene to paper at the next stop—the Indian's expression of resignation as he walked ahead with a rope around his neck, the officers in their frogged British coats and Scotch caps, the troopers in small forage caps.

His vacation was over by this time. He sold his pony to a trapper, loaded some Indian pottery and other souvenirs into his bag, and headed back by wagon and stagecoach to Miles City where he could catch a train. But before he left he selected his favorites among his sketches, stuffed them into an envelope, and addressed them to *Harper's Weekly* in Manhattan.

He arrived home still in his Western clothes and still unshaven. His mother looked at him in disgust. "Get yourself out of those things in a hurry," she commanded him. "Clean yourself up."

Only when he had obeyed her did she give him the letter that had just come for him. It was postmarked New York City. *Harper's Weekly* was buying one of the sketches he had sent. A very small check was enclosed.

He grabbed his mother and swung her around. "Yippee! I'm famous."

She pushed him away. "What are you talking about?"

He waved the check in front of her but she was not impressed. "Hardly enough to compensate for what that trip must have cost you."

The sketch *Harper's* bought, done in pencil on a scrap of brown paper, showed some Montana frontiersmen talking to an Indian. When it finally appeared in the February 25, 1882, issue of the magazine, it bore the title, "Cowboys of Arizona roused by a Scout." Actually Fred had not been in Arizona and there were very few cowboys in Montana simply because there were not yet many cows. Worse ignominy yet, the credit line read, *Drawn by W. A. Rogers from a Sketch by Frederic Remington.* It had been redone by a more experienced Eastern artist!

The trip to Montana had not only showed Fred what he

wanted to do with his life but also restored his health. He had not forgotten Missie, but he decided perhaps it was a good thing he had not married. No married man could lead the kind of life he intended to live, and it seemed to him he would be better off if he cut women out of his life altogether. This was not difficult because all young women outside of Missie still terrified him. He wanted to return West immediately, but his mother insisted he wait.

"You are too young. You have plenty of time."

Though he didn't agree with her he waited—for a year and a half.

CHAPTER · *4*

"This is it, Fred. How do you like it?"

Bob Camp, who had gone to Yale at the same time as Fred and was now a Kansas sheep rancher, had picked Fred up at the Peabody railroad station and now brought his wagon to a halt in front of a small, two-story, unpainted farmhouse.

The gray-brown of its shingles blended with the gray-brown of the prairie, which stretched as far as Fred could see to the overhung gray clouds of the horizon. It did not strike him as being dreary; the finest mansion in the land could not have seemed more beautiful.

"I think it's superb. It's really mine?"

"It's all yours, boy. This here's about the finest grazin' land in the West. Them's the barns and the corral out yonder."

Bob's bad grammar was a conscious mimicry of the local-farmer talk, but his nasal drawl was already natural. Fred remembered him as one of the best-dressed men on the campus. Now, in a faded plaid shirt, old army pants tucked into his boots, a sombrero cocked on the back of his head, and a rather straggly mustache, he looked like any cowboy.

"Folks 'round here don't take much to Eastern dudes," Bob commented, his glance embracing Fred's city clothes. "The sooner you get out of that outfit you're wearing and into some sensible gear, the better off you'll be."

"As you say, boss." Fred grinned and leaped down from the wagon, going around to the back to pull out his bags and the case of canned goods and staples that Bob had advised him to get.

It had started several months before, when a mutual friend had told him where Bob was living. He had written to find out how Bob was doing, and came to the conclusion that he wanted to be a sheepman too. For one thing, unlike cattle ranches, it didn't require a fortune to get started. He had sent a sizable chunk of his inheritance to Bob to purchase three hundred and twenty acres adjoining his own. Now he was ready to launch on a new career, infinitely preferable to working in an office. He felt fine.

"Here, I'll give you a hand," a youth of nineteen with lank sandy hair called from the farmhouse doorway. In two or three long strides he was at Fred's side and, grabbing hold of the case of supplies, hoisted it up on his broad shoulders.

"This is Bill Carr," Bob explained. "He's offered to stick around till you get settled."

"That is, if you ain't got no objections," the youth called back as he headed for the house.

Fred didn't. In fact the one thing he had dreaded was being alone.

The farmhouse into which he followed Bill had only two rooms—a bedroom upstairs and an all-purpose kitchen-dining-

46

living room on the first floor, which was furnished with a few kitchen chairs, a plank table, a single rocking chair and a couch. But in the corner a fire was burning in the coal stove, and from a huge kettle came a pleasant aroma.

"I ain't much of a cook," Bill apologized. "But I allowed as you'd be hungry enough that a luck-of-the-pot stew wouldn't go down badly."

Fred lifted the cover of the kettle to study its unrecognizable contents. "Whatever it is, it's better than I could have done."

They ate on chipped heavy chinaware, using forks with prongs missing and tin knives with rusted handles, but the stew was edible. In between mouthfuls, Bob set forth on the future of the sheep-raising industry in Butler County. He had a herd of nine hundred sheep and expected to get about six to eight thousand pounds of wool that year. Fred would have to put up a sheep shed—there was a good place for one on top of the slope overlooking the range. It wasn't much of a job to look after the sheep in the summer, though it was a man's work to protect the bleating beasts from the blasts of winter weather. Sheep had to be dipped several times a year, a disagreeable but necessary chore. At lambing time they needed constant care, and of course shearing was a man-sized job too. But first he should get a few horses . . .

Fred, who had been only half listening, pricked up his ears. "Of course I want horses. When and where can I get some?"

Bob shrugged. "Tomorrow if you like. Bill and I will go with you to see you don't get taken. They're some shrewd traders around here."

"My Prince," Bill interjected eagerly. "To look at him you'd think he ain't never done nothing but sleep. He's the fastest critter around here except for Push-Bob . . ." He stopped, his fork arrested in mid-air, as hoofbeats echoed. "You got company, Remington."

"Me?" Fred demanded blankly. "I don't know anybody."

"You will," Bob informed him.

There was a knock at the door, but even before Bob's "Come in," it opened.

"How are tricks, boys? I would assume this is Mr. Remington from New York." The undeniably English accent of the new arrival was matched by the perfectly tailored English hunting costume which he wore. He was tall, gangling, broad-faced, with gentle, dark eyes.

"Fred, this is Charlie, who owns a horse ranch seven miles down the creek. He's an Englishman," Bob added unnecessarily.

"I'm the family black sheep," Charlie volunteered with a chuckle. "So they sent me across the seas to raise sheep. Rather amusing, don't you think?"

Bill unobtrusively set another place and filled another cracked plate with his mess of stew.

"Add two more," Charlie suggested. "Our other Plum Grove bachelors are tying up their horses."

His words were followed by a second knock, and two more young men, one very blond and one very dark, stood hesitatingly in the doorway.

"Jim and Johnny," said Bob. "Meet Fred. Jim hails from Illinois and owns Push-Bob, the only horse around here who has a chance against Bill's Prince. Johnny's from Virginia. He's your closest neighbor."

Fred looked around the crowded table in amazement. Bob, Bill, Charlie, Jim, Johnny—five young men of different backgrounds and education, all of whom, like himself, had responded to the challenge of the West. He wasn't going to be alone after all.

They talked endlessly, mostly about horses, specifically about the relative merits of Push-Bob and Prince.

"Why don't you race them and see who wins?" Fred suggested during a lull.

"Never," Bob said with mock horror. "What would be left for us to talk about?"

The next day the five young men escorted Fred on a round of the neighboring ranches to purchase his own horses. He bought several—among them a nervous little half-breed Texas thoroughbred of a beautiful light gold color. Her name was Terra Cotta—Terry for short—and Fred fell in love with her on sight.

Work seemed like play those first weeks on the ranch. Except for Bill, all Fred's new friends had enough money not to worry about it. They spent more time at Fred's ranch than at their own, converting the barns to harbor sheep, fencing in the corral, building a kitchen on his farmhouse, finally negotiating the purchase of several hundred woolly sheep which Fred viewed with a mixture of amusement and disdain. He didn't have the patience to play shepherd to these stupid, docile beasts, a problem he solved by enlisting the services of young boys from neighboring farms.

These youngsters quickly came to worship the blond young giant who had settled in their midst. They spent as much time hanging around the Remington farm as their parents would permit. Unlike the more industrious settlers, Fred always had time for them. He gave them boxing lessons, made them flapjacks, told them stories about faraway Montana, and spent endless hours with them practicing the fine art of throwing a lasso. Sometimes wild-steer-riding contests were held at the ranch. There was always something for the boys to do and see.

One day when they arrived they found Fred sitting out in the middle of the yard on a kitchen stool in front of a makeshift easel, with some water colors at his side. Usually Fred hollered

49

a greeting to them way down the road, but this time he didn't even seem aware of their presence. Silently they gathered around behind him. Before their eyes they saw emerging on the paper tacked at his easel a likeness of Fred's farmhouse, the barns in the background, the old wagon road next to the barn, and even Terra Cotta standing saddled at her hitching post.

Fred's ability to put horses and Texan cattle and sheep on paper impressed these barefoot boys in their patched trousers and cut-down shirts even more than his skill at boxing.

In the evenings the Plum Grove bachelors met either in Fred's or Bob's kitchen, where they ate, drank, sang, and talked far into the night. Sometimes Fred made sketches of them too, with pen and ink or crayon. There were no women in this new life except the farmers' wives who occasionally sent over freshly baked loaves of bread. The other young men sometimes went to Peabody for Saturday-night dances, but Fred would never join them.

Ranching, as Fred did it, was a great deal of fun, but he still regretted the lack of desperadoes and Indians in the peaceful grazing country. Ten years before, the town of Newton, fifteen miles away, had been the center for horse thieves and outlaws, but now the settlers had taken over and the cowboy capital had shifted to Dodge City. Not for anything would Fred have revealed to his friends back in Canton and Ogdensburg that his corner of the Wild West was not as wild as it once had been; his letters home implied that gun fights were a routine occurrence on the streets of Peabody.

In place of scouting after "Injuns" or riding down outlaws, Fred's friends decided to take him rabbit coursing, or "running the jacks" as the local folk put it. This consisted in riding over the prairie and trying to get near enough to a rabbit to touch it with a long sick.

"Six grown men and six horses after one little rabbit?" Fred scoffed as they discussed the plan the night before at Bob's ranch.

"Don't forget the dogs," Bob grinned, patting his lame mongrel. "Peg-leg here will go along. So will Johnny's greyhound, Daddy. They'll do more work than we do."

Though Fred sneered at the tameness of the sport, he was up before dawn the next morning, riding Terra Cotta across the fields to meet the others—Bill Carr on Prince and Jim on Push-Bob, Johnny riding a big bay, and Bob with his dependable mare, Jane. Charlie, impeccably dressed as always, rode a blue mare. At the last moment Phil, a little, dark, wiry youth who cooked for Bob, decided to join them. Since he was frightened of horses, he rode a gray mule.

Everything started out fine. A light haze hung over the land, and as Terra Cotta swept up the bluffs and over the range, brushing dew from the grass, Fred felt her stride under him like taut steel. He felt wonderful.

"There's a jack. Take him, Daddy!" Johnny cried suddenly.

The others caught just a glimpse of the rabbit as the greyhound tore after her into the long grass. Jim spurred Push-Bob after them through a ravine linked with willows. Push-Bob headed for the willows which brushed Jim neatly from his back.

The incident set the pattern for the rest of the morning. By noon they had all been dismounted one or more times. Their score against the rabbits was zero. They assembled to discuss the situation. Bob's Jane had tumbled him into a mudpool. Fred commented that he looked as though he had been dipped in plaster. The others were not in much better shape and all were famished.

"What do you say we call it a day?" Johnny suggested. "Lady Luck seem to have a grudge against us."

No one objected and they headed homeward. But with some ten miles still to go, another rabbit crossed their path, and

51

horses, men, and dogs were after it. To their sorrow the rabbit dived under a fence into a corral to vanish forever from their lives.

The corral belonged to a newcomer to the neighborhood, a crotchety old man with scraggly side whiskers called John Mitchener. He ambled out.

"Howdy, boys. Need some help?"

"I suppose you think you could track down more rabbits than we have," Jim said disgustedly.

The old man took a leisurely puff at his corncob pipe. "I reckon as how I might if I had that cowskin horse I owned back in Missouri . . ."

John's "cowskin horse" was already a legend in Plum Grove, and nobody really believed there was such an animal.

"I'll tell you something, Uncle John," Jim said with an air of innocence. "The other day I met a chap from Missouri who allowed as how he once bet your cowskin hoss with a mule!"

"What do you mean, he bet my hoss with a mule?" Old John exploded indignantly. "That fellow's a liar!"

"Mebbe you're right, Uncle John," Johnny interrupted soothingly. "I saw the Missouri chap too. I thought he wasn't telling the truth, but I didn't tell him so because he had red eyes and was loaded with guns."

"Don't try to fool an old man like me," Old John sputtered. "Get off your hosses and come inside, the lot of you. It's time for grub."

"Well, thanks, Uncle John."

The old fellow wasn't so mean after all, Fred reflected as he, with the others, dismounted and tied his mount to the corral fence. They followed him into the kitchen where his boy, or hired hand, was preparing bacon and eggs. The food smelled good but they were doomed not to taste it. This was because Jim was such a great tease—and didn't know when to stop once he got started.

"Uncle John," he said, tipping back in one of the rickety chairs, "from what I see you ain't got a hoss in your corral that you could bet a Mexican quarter on."

Old John refused to rise to the bait. "You're right there. My stock now ain't nothing to brag about," he agreed. "I got one little mare though I reckon is a smarter critter than any of those you boys hitched to my fence."

Fred and Bob exchanged winks, and Jim said mockingly, "Why, Uncle John, my Push-Bob or Bill Carr's Prince would shuffle sand into your mare's eyes in no time."

Old John pulled himself to his feet slowly. "Ain't no time like the present fer decidin' such matters. If your horse beats mine, you kin have her."

"You're on." Jim rose too, his eyes gleaming.

Bill wanted to be in on it too. "I'll bet Prince can beat either of you. S'pose we all three run and the winner'll take both."

All of them filed out, including Old John's boy, leaving bacon and eggs to burn to a crisp.

John's mare, when he led her out, proved to be so ancient and decrepit they saw they were really up against a sure thing. Fred put up Terra Cotta against another mare and colt in John's corral. Bob bet Jane against four head of John's cattle. Johnny entered his horse, and Charlie staked his blue mare against a three-year-old in the old man's string of horses. Only Phil bet nothing on his mule.

The old man removed his shirt. Jim and Bill took off their jackets and shoes, and substituted handkerchiefs tied around their heads for their sombreros. Fred fired the shot and the race was on. Bill and Jim rode their steeds like centaurs, but Old John, his gray hair and beard flowing in the breeze, went to the front and stayed there till the end, winning by several

53

lengths. Prince and Push-Bob arrived neck to neck; no one could see which was best. Nor did it matter now.

The six young men stood disconsolately at the fence of the corral as Old John herded in his newly acquired string. "Perhaps ye'll have more faith in cowskin-horse stories now, Mr. Jim," he said, "seeing as this here gray mare of mine is herself known back in Missouri as the original cowskin horse. I'll tell ye the particulars 'bout her if you want to come back and finish your dinner."

But no one was eager for dinner or particulars, and packing their six empty saddles on the back of Phil's mule, they started the long trek back to their various ranches.

Two days later Fred and Bill Carr—on different mounts—rode to Hoyt's grocery store at Plum Grove for supplies. Through the window they caught sight of Old John perched on a sugar barrel, with an audience that seemed to include every settler in the vicinity. At the climax of his story a shout of laughter exploded that might have been heard in Peabody. The two young men looked wordlessly at each other and then turned and rode away empty-handed.

The clear October days changed to a gray November and a December of wintry blasts. The youngsters who had guarded the sheep in the summer were at school now, and it was up to Fred to protect the bleating animals from the biting winds and snow. It was work—more than he had bargained for.

By February he had had all he could take. He had a chance to travel down to southwest Kansas with a friend from Peabody, and he took advantage of the offer in a hurry, leaving Bill in charge of his sheep. At the state border he left his friend and continued on his own into Indian Territory, where he hired a cowboy driver with a wagon and a couple of sad-looking ponies to drive him to Fort Reno. Though the Territory had been granted to the Indians by a government treaty, already the Oklahoma boomers were launching a campaign to have it opened to settlers. Fred wanted to see it before this happened.

For some miles they followed a creek shaded with post oak and pecan trees, stopping at dinnertime to rest their horses. The fee Fred had agreed to pay was supposed to include meals, but when he saw the "vittles" the driver took from a greasy newspaper he decided he was not hungry. Still and all he was content. He was seeing a new kind of country, one not yet overrun by the white man. He didn't even mind when a little later one of the ponies balked at a small hill and he had to get out and push the wagon until the animal could be coaxed to resume its haulage. Nor was he worried when the road became so covered with sand that they lost it altogether. After all, it was an adventure of a sort.

They struggled forward until they came to a group of wretched lean-tos.

"Caddoes," warned the driver. "They may be hostile."

But there were only two of this once-proud tribe in evidence, and they were so indifferent to the approach of the white men that they didn't bother to get up from the framework of poles on which they were taking their siesta.

The driver talked to them first in English and then in sign language, but it took a handful of change to make them understand. After some hard bargaining the younger of the two roused himself to saddle his horse and show them the way. He led them to the South Canadian River by sunset; when they had crossed its wide sand bars and shallow waters only a red gleam was left in the western sky. They made camp about a mile from the flickering lights of an Arapahoe campfire. Fred and the driver stretched out on the grass bank and munched kernels of the same corn they had fed the horses to still their hunger, while the Caddo sat upright on his pony.

They were startled by the sound of horses' hoofs. Before any of them could move, one of the Arapahoes rode up. The Caddo saluted him and for a full half-hour they talked. Though both their signs and their speech were incomprehensible to Fred, he watched in fascination. The Arapahoe, an old man with noble profile clearly outlined against the fading twilight sky, was dressed in full regalia with leggings, beaded moccasins, and a sheet wrapped about his waist and thighs. The Caddo, in contrast, had adopted modern dress—boots, a cowboy's oilskin coat, his hair cropped short.

What a painting they would make, Fred thought dreamily— this parley on horseback between the old and the new Indian. It should be in oils to catch the purple and reddish shadows of the night, and above all it must reveal the animal grace of their gestures and movements. Sometime he would do it—but not now; he was not ready yet. He went to sleep with the strange scene etched permanently in some far corner of his consciousness.

The next day found them at Fort Reno, where Fred presented himself to the colonel in charge, explaining that he was an artist and wished to visit the nearby Cheyenne reservation.

The colonel studied him so suspiciously that Fred became aware of his unshaven, disreputable appearance. Then the man guffawed. "An artist, eh? I thought you was a Texas horse thief." The scrutiny over, he called in an interpreter, whom he introduced as "Ben Clark, the best Cheyenne scout in the country." He was a tall, dark-haired young man in shining boots, riding breeches, dark tie and shirt, and cowboy hat, who didn't look at all like an Indian. But he proved to be an excellent guide.

They rode out of the fort in a buckboard hitched to a pair of mules supplied by the quartermaster. They met other Cheyennes as they crossed the plains, men almost as tall as Fred with fine, strong features, hair in braids, all using light cow saddles, long stirrups, and no spurs.

The reservation was a group of canvas lodges and tents in the midst of a prairie of waving grass. The Cheyennes knew Ben as a friend and bantered with him while Fred wandered around trying to take in the strange scenes: a medicine man working over a sick youth, children playing with dogs, a group of young men preparing for a clan dance, women beading moccasins. He sketched a very ancient Indian with gray hair and a thousand wrinkles and, for variety, a pretty young woman in a calico robe, who ran off laughing when Ben told her what Fred was doing.

Next, Ben took him to meet the chief of the lodge, a man of enormous dignity and reserve. When Ben told him Fred was an artist, the chief looked bewildered. "For Indians the white race is divided into three parts," Ben explained to Fred: "soldiers, Texas cowboys, and the Big Chief from Washington. You are none of the three." Nevertheless the chief consented to put on his war dress and let Fred sketch him.

They spent three days at the reservation, which gave Fred a chance to witness the roundup of cattle for branding, the Indians riding after and throwing the steer allocated to each, and to talk with young and old alike, with Ben as translator, on the problems that interested them most: the likelihood of the government reversing the terms of the treaty; the insufficiency of the food ration; the futility of white men's schools for their youth who returned unable to readapt to Indian life and yet were not allowed to live as white men did. It was the first time Fred had ever heard the Indian's viewpoint.

After that experience he headed down through Texas, stopping long enough to go quail hunting with a contingent of soldiers and to visit a very old colonel with a long white beard who had been with the Texas Rangers at the Alamo. At the border he crossed over into Chihuahua and found himself a new love in this land of adobe huts and Mexican *vaqueros* and vast stretches of plains and mountains. Mexico, he decided there and then, was also part of his West, and, as such, also a subject for his paintbrush. He would have liked to stay longer, but he was, after all, a rancher with responsibilities. He returned by stagecoach, stopping only for a brief visit to the rowdy town of Dodge City.

He arrived back at the farm with his hair bleached and his face burned by the southern sun and wind, and with grim determination settled down to the chores of dipping his sheep and mothering them through their lambing period. When spring came he hired a crew to shear them, and got quite a thrill out of riding around supervising the job. But the price of wool took a big slump that year of 1884. The profits were not what he had anticipated in his rosier dreams. It became obvious to him that he was no more equipped to run a sheep ranch successfully than he was to work as a clerk. Shortly thereafter he sold the ranch to a man named D. M. Greene and set off for Kansas City.

Before he left he made a sketch for Phil, Bob's cook, of a cow defending a calf from an attack of wolves, and the last thing he did was to go inside the barn and cut on the wall with a knife a drawing of a cowboy roping a steer. It was his mark on the farm where he had known exultation, boredom, good fellowship, and drudgery.

CHAPTER 5

The sale of his ranch in March of 1884 left Fred footloose and with money in his pocket again. The practical side of his nature told him he should invest in some business to ensure his future. Ostensibly to find some such opportunity he set out on another tour, through Colorado and Wyoming, traveling sometimes by stagecoach or wagon train, sometimes on horseback. His original reason for the trap was soon forgotten. He found it more pleasurable to follow the trails of the original explorers than to discuss business.

Businessmen all looked alike to him, as did most women except Missie, but when it came to horses and men of the outdoors, his sense of observation was wonderfully acute. He made innumerable sketches on this trip, and what they lacked in technical perfection was made up for by the accuracy of their reporting. What was even more valuable perhaps was that he learned to plan pictures from the stories he was told.

One night he bunked at a line camp with an old cowboy, a forlorn sort of character with long, droopy mustaches and a faraway expression in his pale blue eyes. When he took off his hat, Fred noted that he was completely bald, a more unusual sight among outdoor men than among city dwellers.

"I suppose you be wondering what happened to my hair," the cowboy drawled as they shared a meal of beans and sourdough biscuit.

Fred shrugged. "It's none of my business."

"Nope. It ain't." The cowboy ate in silence for a few moments, wiping up the beans with the remains of the biscuit. Then, as he lit up his old pipe, he said, "I was just barely ten when it happened."

Fred waited. The best way to get a man to talk about his past was not to press him.

It had happened when he was ten, the cowboy repeated. He had come out with his folks and another family in a covered wagon a quarter of a century before. "The West warn't like it is now." How often Fred had heard that. "It was real wild-like, still big herds of buffaloes. Hardly any farms. Lots of Indians. One day on the Kansas plains they swooped down on us, Blackfeet I guess they was, giving out them war whoops, stampeding the oxen into a creek and shootin' arrows. My pa and ma, the other family, the drivers, they was all killed. I tried to fight back with a long stick." He stopped and puffed hard on his pipe.

"They scalped me and left me for dead," he resumed presently. "No one is supposed to live after bein' scalped, but I was a tough one. An old trader found me and took care of me till I was able to get around again. But there warn't no way of growin' hair on the top of my head after that."

Fred could see the event as clearly as though he had been there himself—the long procession of covered wagons, the Indians on their ponies wearing their feathered bonnets, the little boy standing defiantly, knee-deep in the creek, a long stick in his hand. He knew someday he would make a painting of it. He would call it "The Emigrants," and it would show people what it was like in the old days as no other work of fiction or fact could possibly do.

Another day, he passed two riders on the trail, an Indian in war dress with a long spear on the end of which was a scalp, and a white man. Both carried rifles. A third horse, fully saddled, was between them. Their faces was stolid and they didn't respond to Fred's greeting.

He speculated about them later. What was their relationship? Was the white a squaw-man who had gone to live with the Indians, and had they together murdered some lone rider and stolen his horse? Or had their meeting been entirely by chance, and were they continuing together because neither trusted the other if they separated? He memorized every detail of their attire and their expressions. He would call this painting "Questionable Companionship," and those who saw it could make their own guesses.

Water holes had a fascination for Fred. They were wide apart in the cactus country of New Mexico. The Indians knew them all and soldiers, prospectors, or other travelers had to stop at them to fill their canteens and water their horses. Each water hole had been the setting of a hundred dramatic incidents of the past. At one of them he met a veteran who told him how, some years before, he and five or six other soldiers had been surprised by some Indians when they were watering their horses, and how they had fought them until all were wounded.

Fred encouraged him to show just where he and the others had been standing and where their horses had fallen. He painted that picture too, very many years later, calling it "Fight for the Waterhole." After it was published, he received a letter from the chief of police at Abilene. He remembered the place very well, but he didn't see how Fred could have described it so realistically. He could vouch for this realism becaues he had been one of the soldiers.

The days passed and Fred, loaded with sketches and souvenirs, eventually drifted back to Kansas City. There he rented a small house, bought a supply of paints and canvas and an easel from an art dealer named William Findlay, and set himself to use his sketches as the basis for finished drawings and paintings such as could not be done on the road.

Kansas City was a rough, sprawling, overgrown village at that

61

time, with a good sprinkling of plain, honest citizens and a large percentage of speculators, gamblers, blackmailers, and others out to make an easy dollar. It also had its quota of society folk who lived in big and often ugly mansions and had clothes and furniture shipped from New York.

There was the beginning of a cultural movement in the town. It was a matter of civic pride that the kindly Irish-born artist, John Mulvaney, had painted his "Custer's Last Rally" in Kansas City in 1881, and there was talk in the newspapers of the development of a distinctive Western form of art.* It was not long until these culturally-minded citizens heard that a new young artist was in their midst, and occasionally they visited him and even more occasionally paid him a few dollars for a painting.

After one or two experiments, however, Fred refused invitations to dinner or tea from such wealthy sponsors, preferring the company he found in the local saloons. It was a long time since his fourteen-year-old resolution never to take a drink. In the West a man had to take a drink or be thought a weakling. At twenty-two, in spite of his hardy physique, Fred still had a boyish face. Drinking was one way of proving himself a man, or at least so he thought. He learned to be a good poker player in those days too, occasionally got into boxing bouts—usually to the detriment of his opponent—and sometimes dawn would find him riding with a crony out to the edge of town lassooing sunflowers. He made friends with odd characters: George Gaston, a former Bavarian colonel who was a connoisseur of art and roast beef and spoke five languages; and the equally colorful Sheriff Charlie Bennett who tended bar when he was off-duty.

* The more famous "Custer's Last Fight," by Cassilly Adams, which was lithographed by Otto Becker and reproduced throughout America, was not yet in existence when Remington was in Kansas.

Though the male population of Kansas City still far exceeded the female, Fred's good looks and friendly, open manner would have made it easy for him to find a girl, had he wanted to. He didn't and went to all extremes to avoid feminine entanglements. One day on the street he met a young lady and her brother whom he had seen at one of the fancy teas he had been induced to attend during his first weeks in the city.

"Oh, Mr. Remington," the young lady gushed. "I've been wondering what happened to you. Why don't we ever see you any more?"

Fred looked at her blankly, then turned and bolted into a restaurant, where he sometimes ate when he wasn't in the mood to open a can for his own dinner.

"I'm in a spot. Help me out," he pleaded to the proprietor.

A moment later the young lady and her brother, standing at the restaurant entrance, saw Fred dressed in a white apron busily polishing the brass on the bar. They turned and left.

It finally occurred to Fred that the only way to avoid women permanently was to change Missie's mind about marrying him. But to do that he had to show her father that he was able to support her.

Such an opportunity unexpectedly fell into his lap, or so it seemed. The owners of a saloon on West Sixth Street called Bishop and Christie's, where he was a frequent visitor, suggested he might like to buy a third interest as a silent partner.

"We've had plenty of offers," they told him. "But we have to be careful. We don't want no Eastern gentleman telling us how to run our business."

Fred was flattered and delighted. As long as there were men in the West, he figured, there would be need for whisky. As a "silent partner" he could take in his share of the profits and continue to work at his painting. They made a gentlemen's agreement, and he turned over to his two new partners practically all that was left of his inheritance from his father.

A few weeks later he decided to drop in and see how his investment was coming along. There were no lights and the wooden door was nailed shut. His banging and shouting brought no response except for the appearance of a scrawny adolescent kid from around the corner.

"Lookin' for something, Mister?"

"I'm looking for the owners," Fred bellowed.

The boy stared at him with the contempt and pity of a youth toward a drunken elder. "They're gone."

Fred felt panic in his throat. "What do you mean, gone?"

"Moved out. Gave a big party before they left. Free drinks for everyone. It was great. Six men got thrown out."

"Do you know where they went, son?" Fred asked, trying to keep his temper under control.

"Sure I know. They moved to Delaware Street. Got a bigger place there." The youth started to move off. "Don't take any wooden nickels," he called over his shoulder with a snicker.

Fred hardly heard him. If they had just moved to another part of the city, his investment was still safe. But why hadn't they told him? It was one thing to be a silent partner in a growing enterprise, but quite a different matter to be a neglected one.

He found the address on Delaware Street without too much difficulty. It was indeed a larger place than the other, with a fine new bar of polished wood, and fancy chandeliers. His money had gone into that, he reflected as he stormed in, ready to do battle.

One of the owners was there to greet him. "Howdy there, Fred. It's sure good to see you. How about a drink?"

"No thanks," said Fred, ignoring the outstretched hand. "I came to talk."

64

Why sure, Fred. Sit down at a table in the back and I'll be with you in just a moment."

But it was quite a long time that he left Fred fuming impatiently, and when he returned he had his partner in tow.

"You ready for that drink yet, Fred?"

"No," Fred said shortly. "Why didn't you tell me you were moving?"

"To tell the truth, you weren't around to tell. Too bad you couldn't come to our farewell party. It was great."

"I heard about it." Fred's voice was grim. "You knew my address."

"Well, you know how it is. We ain't much on writing letters to customers, my partner and me."

"You seem to forget that I'm a partner too," Fred said loudly. "I have a third interest in this place and I intend to get something out of it."

"Come now, Fred. That's not the way to act among friends. Our—er—clientele might think something was wrong. What's all this talk about a third interest anyway? You got papers to prove it?"

Fred hadn't. They had a "gentleman's agreement." What a chump he had been. "Why you . . ." He stood up, with his hands clenched.

"I wouldn't do that if I was you," the man said warningly. "I want you to meet a pal of mine."

Fred looked up furiously to see a giant of a man, full six inches taller than he was, and all muscle.

"This is Abraham, Freddie. He's our new bouncer. We call him Ape for short. He threw out six people at our farewell party, three under each arm. I'd advise you to leave, son. We don't allow no drunks in here now. Will you go on your own legs, or do you want Ape here to help you?"

All around men were turning to stare curiously. Fred tightened his lips. "I'll be back," he said as he turned to walk out.

"Hope you will, Freddie boy," his ex-partner smiled. "Glad to see you any time."

Blind with rage, Fred half ran, half stumbled to his house. From a dresser drawer he took out his Colt revolver, put aside for his period of "peaceful" residence, and dashed back to the saloon, taking up a stand not far from the doors.

One by one the customers left, but still there was no sign of the owners or even of Ape. The lights went out. He continued to wait. It wasn't until dawn that he realized they had expected him and left by a back door.

He was there again later in the morning, his hand on his holster. He hadn't slept, and anger was still his master. They had to appear sometime. He would wait until they did. But by noon the saloon was still closed. No one had shown up.

"Good morning, Mr. Remington."

Fred turned around with a start, automatically pulling out his gun. But the man with the soft brown mustache who addressed him had a mild look and was dressed in a business suit and a celluloid collar. Fred recognized him as a Mr. Hall, who had once been brought over to his home to look at his paintings. He hadn't bought any but had expressed the hope he would someday be able to.

"Oh . . . good morning." Fred suddenly felt foolish standing there in the midst of Kansas City's midday traffic, acting like a character in a dime novel.

"Nice day." It was true. The sun was shining and the air was fresh. Fred hadn't noticed before.

"You seem upset about something," Mr. Hall commented. He had noticed the holster and the gun then. "I don't suppose you'd want to talk about it."

"I think I do," Fred said. He blurted out the whole sad story.

"Well, if it's only a question of money, it's not so serious," the little man said consolingly. "Only I think, Mr. Remington, you're going about this the wrong way. If you shoot these men, you'd end up in jail, possibly on trial for murder. This is a modern town, you know. It isn't like the old days. There are lawyers to take care of this sort of thing. Suppose you come with me and we'll talk it over."

Fred found himself being propelled along the streets to Mr. Hall's home, a simple frame place like his own but with patches of flowers around the porch, indicating a woman somewhere in the background.

"Oh, Nellie," Mr. Hall called out as they entered the front door. "Come on in. I've brought a visitor."

A pleasant-looking woman with soft graying hair made her appearance.

"This is Mr. Remington, a newspaperman from New York. He's having dinner with us."

"How very nice to meet you." Mrs. Hall held out her hand. "How big you are. I thought for a moment you were a gunman, but now I see you're very young."

Her words didn't offend Fred; he liked her immediately. "I'm glad to meet you too, ma'am." This sane and homey atmosphere, after the nightmare of the last fifteen hours, was curiously unreal. He hoped he didn't look as nervous as he felt.

"Mr. Remington has just had a most unpleasant experience," Mr. Hall announced a little later as they were consuming his wife's fluffy mashed potatoes and pork chops. "He has lost all his money in a bad investment."

"What a pity," cried Mrs. Hall. "We'll have to get a lawyer to get it back, won't we?"

"We'll try," Mr. Hall said.

Fred laid down his fork and looked from one to the other.

"I think I've just had an attack of madness," he burst out. "Mrs. Hall, your husband has probably saved my life."

"Oh, come now," she said soothingly. "It probably wasn't as bad as that. Do have a second helping, Mr. Remington. You look as if you could use a mite of home cooking."

He became a frequent visitor at their house after that. Through Mr. Hall he got a lawyer, but it didn't do him much good. The trick that had been played on him was a rather common one with unscrupulous businessmen of this period. Without legal papers there was really nothing that could be done.

Fred needed money to live on. He persuaded Mr. Findlay, the man who ran the store where he bought his art supplies, to come look at his work.

"I may be making a mistake, but I'll pay you a hundred dollars for the lot and see if I can sell any."

Fred jumped at the offer.

The money kept him going for a few weeks, and Mr. Findlay reported that several of his pictures had been sold. He told him that one of his clients had requested a duplicate of one of them.

"Of course I'll make it for him," Fred offered eagerly.

Mr. Findlay shook his head. "Take my advice, young man. Never repeat. Whenever a picture is duplicated it loses one half of its value. Give him another one. He'll buy it."

The art dealer's prophesy proved correct. After this sale Fred had just enough money to get back to New York with a few dollars to spare.

A couple of weeks later he was walking up the path to the Caten house in Gloversville. Missie came to the door in answer to his knock. She was dressed in pale blue with a little black shawl over her shoulders and she was even prettier than he remembered her.

"Yes?" she asked.

68

With a start Fred realized she didn't recognize him. It wasn't surprising. He was taller and broader than the youth of nineteen who had courted her so desperately. The sun and hot winds had reddened and roughened his skin. He had grown a thick mustache, as blond as the rest of his hair. Even his city clothes, now too tight across the shoulders, didn't disguise the fact that he was no longer an Easterner.

"You don't remember me, Missie?"

She stared at him blankly, and then suddenly opened the door for him.

They sat for hours in the parlor talking, the family with rare tact not intruding. Later the two of them went to face Mr. Caten in his study.

"Father, you remember Mr. Remington," Missie said in the clear, sweet voice Fred knew so well. "He has just come back from the West. We are going to be married and I am going to live in Kansas City with him. If you refuse, I will run away with him."

Fred waited for the expected explosion. It didn't come.

"You have a home out there, young man?" Mr. Caten asked, tapping his desk with his fingers.

"Yes, sir. I think Eva will be happy."

"Well, that's fine." The older man smiled almost apologetically. "I've long since learned it's quite impossible for me to make up my daughters' minds. They do what they want anyway."

That was all there was to it. No questions were asked about his present or future prospects. They were married on his birthday, October 1, 1884, almost four years after Mr. Caten had rejected him as a suitor for his daughter. No mention was made of the fact that at that time Fred had been a young man with an inheritance, while he was now a young man who was penniless.

As a wedding gift Fred's Uncle William gave them enough money to get back to Kansas. On their arrival Mr. Findlay came to see them and announced that in Fred's absence he had sold one of his paintings of some mounted plainsmen for 250 dollars, which sum he insisted on turning over to them. It was an auspicious beginning to married life.

Missie seemed delighted with Fred's little house and set to work scrubbing and cleaning as though she had been accustomed to such hard work all her life. Fred found out that in addition to her other virtues, she had a good disposition, was patient with his moods of depression, and was quiet, unassuming, and modest. He took Missie to see the Halls, who were charmed with her, as was indeed everyone who met her.

Winter set in, cold and damp and dreary. Sometimes the badly heated house was so chilly that Fred could hardly hold his paintbrush. His numerous friends, who had kept out of sight the first weeks of their marriage, began to stray in, often as not at mealtime. Missie never seemed to mind setting the table for unexpected guests, no matter how rough their appearance or crude their manners.

The money from Findlay dwindled with appalling rapidity. He had new hope when *Harper's* bought a second drawing, "Ejecting an Oklahoma Boomer," which he had first sketched when he had taken the trip down to Indian Territory. But when it finally appeared, like the first there was another name on the byline: *Drawn by T. Thulstrup from a Sketch by Frederic Remington.* It seemed as though they would never find him good enough to do his own work.

The old coal range in the kitchen, as though to protest against the Kansas weather, started to smoke and clog. One day Fred came in to find Missie in tears. The fire had gone out in the middle of her baking, and a whole batch of bread was ruined.

"It's a little thing," Fred tried to comfort her. "It's not worth one of your tears."

"I know it's a little thing," she said mournfully. "It's just that there are so many little things."

With horror he realized what he was subjecting her to—this gently bred girl who had all her life been accustomed to luxury. When he tried to sympathize with her, she protested, with an abrupt return of good spirits, that she had never been so happy in her life. She stuck it out until the next summer. With fall approaching again, Fred couldn't help noticing that she seemed quieter, more subdued. He urged her to return to Gloversville for a visit to her family. He would remain out West for the time being, and as soon as things picked up he would come and get her. It wouldn't be for long. She refused obstinately at first; finally and very reluctantly she agreed to go. "But only for a short while, Fred."

After she was gone, he gave up his house and moved in with the Halls. Nice as they were to him, he felt lost and defeated. Just occasionally his old spirit showed up.

"Why don't you do a picture of my baby?" Mrs. Hall suggested one day when he was wandering around restlessly.

"You'd never speak to me again if I did," he said, grinning. "I nearly lost Missie that way last winter. I made her pose for me and the result was an old Indian squaw. I'd be sure to turn your baby into a papoose."

He did get Mr. Hall to pose for him for a picture called "Sentinels on Guard." Mr. Hall, who was city-bred and knew nothing about guns, was, in turn, all the sentinels in that picture which he gave to the Halls in return for their hospitality.

Then one day he had a visitor from the East—the last person in the world he would have expected to brave the rigors of frontier life—his own mother.

"I had to come, Fred," she explained when Mrs. Hall diplomatically left them alone in the dining room. "I've been upset about you. It's just as I thought, isn't it? You don't have a job, do you? You've lost your inheritance, haven't you? Fred, it's time you gave up this nonsense and came home. Your father's friends will still help you get a steady position. You have a wife to think of now."

She was perfectly right in everything she said. She made Fred feel very guilty. But he couldn't do as she asked. "I'm sorry, Mother. When I can I'll go back, but I'm not ready yet. Missie will understand."

"Well, I've tried. That's all I can say," his mother said resignedly. She left the following day without even asking to see any of his work.

A week or so later Fred returned from town riding a lean gray mare. He called the Halls out to see her.

"Her name is Mathilde," he said with a familiar sparkle in his eyes. "She and I are going to start out for the Southwest tomorrow and see if we can rustle up a little gold. I've got to get rich some way."

CHAPTER · *6*

A prospector carries on his pack hoss or mule everything he needs for the days or weeks or months he is in the mountains or out in the desert. His supplies are not extensive: bacon, flour, coffee, sugar, tobacco, pick, shovel, frying pan, coffee pot, roll of blankets, and a gun and ammunition to provide him fresh meat or fowl on occasion. Fred had all of these, in addition to sketch pads and portfolio. Still, he would have been at a loss had

72

he not had the good fortune to meet up with two oldtimers who had just about run out of "grub." He shared his with them in exchange for lessons on the best places to dig, the outcroppings that were most likely to produce valuable ore, and other professional secrets.

The region around the Pinal Range in Arizona was full of stories of gold. There was the fabulously rich mine allegedly discovered by a Negro named Seminole Bill, who had subsequently disappeared. There was the legend of another mine, guarded by Apaches, it was said, where death awaited any white man who ventured near. Fred's two new friends were convinced that sooner or later they, too, would find untold wealth. This hope had sustained them through all the hardships and danger of their chosen way of life.

Fred didn't mind the danger. Living within a stone's throw of death appealed to him, or at least he thought it did.

The three of them were sitting around their campfire one evening smoking and telling stories.

"Hear what happened over yonder the other day?" asked one of the prospectors, a rugged old fellow whom Fred knew only as Ben. "A band of Apaches scalped forty-eight white men."

"That right?" Fred assumed a nonchalance he was far from feeling. "I suppose it was Geronimo's outfit."

"Naw." Ben let out a snort of disdain. "Geronimo's over in the Sierra Madres in Mexico. He wouldn't dare come around here. Not with Captain Crawford and his men out looking for him."

"I heard different," broke in the other prospector, who called himself Angus, a little man weathered far beyond his years by the fierce Arizona sun. "I heard he come back over the border and was keeping his eye on Crawford's men. They'll never catch up with him. He's too dang smart for them."

Fred felt his spine tingle. It was an eerie thought that savage

Indians were lurking somewhere nearby in the star-filled night. "We should wipe them all out," he exploded.

"I dunno," drawled Ben. "Seems to me there's two ways of lookin' at every question. The way the Indians look at it, we ain't got no right to be here at all."

"The fact is we're here to stay and the sooner they know it, the better," Fred said morosely.

"Sure," said Ben, "but sometimes one can't help thinkin'. Ever hear how Geronimo came to be mad at white men? They say when he was young he and his tribe went down to Mexico to do some friendly trading and just sort of take a vacation. There was a Mexican general there named Carasco who didn't like Indians, and when the men were off trading he had all the women and young 'uns shot. Seems Geronimo found his wife and three little boys killed by that Mexican general."

"What a rotten thing to do!" Fred's anger transferred itself to the Mexican general. "That is, if it's true."

"Mebbe yes, mebbe no." Ben spat into the fire. "I'm just tellin' what I heard."

They lapsed into silence, laying back on the ground and staring up at the stars, each man thinking his own thoughts. For some reason Fred sat up—and gaped in astonishment. At the opposite side of the fire three Apaches were sitting, their rifles on their laps. He would have thought he was dreaming except that Ben and Angus spied them at the same moment, and he heard their low whistles of amazement.

"Heap hungry," one of their visitors remarked.

The three men jumped to their feet, reaching for their guns. The Indian who had first spoken raised his hand palm forward in a gesture of peace. "No want fight. Want flour."

With a nod from the two prospectors, Fred ladled out some flour into a container, adding a slab of bacon for good measure. As the visitors still made no move to go, he served them the

74

remains of the rabbit stew that had been their supper. The Indians ate solemnly, then stretched themselves out on the ground and went to sleep.

Ben and Angus did the same, but for Fred there was little sleep. The Indians seemed amazing un-sinister, but maybe it was a trick and the rest of the tribe would presently drop from the trees. It was both a relief and a let-down that nothing more happened; at dawn the redmen took their leave and vanished toward the distant hills.

Later in the day as Fred and his two companions were riding down a narrow canyon, an idea struck him: "Either of you know what Geronimo looks like?"

"Nope," they said.

"I wonder . . ." He didn't finish his sentence. He didn't need to. All the rest of his life he would be trying to convince himself that one of their three uninvited visitors was the ferocious Indian chieftain.

He stayed with Ben and Angus a few more days and then took leave of them, their mules, and prospecting forever. Looking for gold, he had learned, was even greater drudgery than raising sheep. Maybe they would find their bonanza one day. He knew he wouldn't. He had neither their faith nor their patience.

He headed North and later in the day, on a small promontory overlooking the plains, he drew his horse to a halt. It was not cold though the sky was gray and overcast, contrasting harmoniously with the soft browns and orange red of the Southwest sand and rocks. The stillness and beauty moved him deeply.

He imagined a group of Indians watching from this spot as a train of covered wagons approached in the far distance, and he tried to conceive what those Indians would be thinking. It was no use. He could see them with their strong, impressive faces, but he could not think like them.

He blinked his eyes in amazement. The covered wagons he had conjured up in his imagination seemed actually to be taking form. At least something was stirring where there had been only empty stretches of sand and cactus before. He sat motionless on his horse as the moving line grew larger and nearer. Then he almost laughed out loud. It was not a covered-wagon train but a troop of cavalry. Gradually he made out the Indian scouts at the front, Apaches he judged them by their long, dark hair and headbands over their foreheads, then the mounted officers and men, and finally the pack mules at the rear, headed by the "bell mare," the horse chosen to lead the way for the mules.

He turned his own mare and spurred her on, hurrying down the winding trail as though to greet long-lost friends.

The Apache scouts gazed at him curiously as, with a gesture of greeting, he drew his horse to the side to let them pass and waited for the cavalry. They were a weary-looking lot, their uniforms dust-encrusted, lines of fatigue etched in their features, their eyes bloodshot, sitting grimly upright in their saddles as though held there by a stubbornness that defied the laws of human endurance. Fred, looking at them objectively as an artist, felt a sudden thrill. These were the men he wanted to record with his paintbrush—not the smart soldiers one saw on parade in the East.

A lieutenant about Fred's age, his young face haggard and gray as though he had not slept for weeks, pulled up his reins.

"You a prospector, Mister?"

"I made a stab at it over the Pinal Range way," Fred said.

"Did you see any hostiles?"

Fred shook his head. "Only three who came to our camp one night begging for food. I thought one of them might be Geronimo, but now it doesn't seem likely."

"Anything is possible," said the lieutenant. "Geronimo seems to be everywhere—and nowhere. We've been six weeks on his trail and haven't seen hide nor hair of him or any of his gang. It's like tracking down a phantom."

"Mind if I tag along for a few days?" Fred asked.

The lieutenant stared at him in amazement. "Whatever for?"

"Well, I'm an artist. I'd like to make some sketches of your men . . ."

"You want to draw us?" the lieutenant demanded incredulously. "Can't you find prettier things to paint?"

Fred grinned. "Like bowls of flowers? Maybe. Seriously, what I want most is to show the folks back East what the army does out here—what it's really like."

"That's a new one, Mister. I'll tell you the truth. We call ourselves the forgotten army. No one seems to have the slightest interest in us."

"Then it's all right if I stay around long enough to find out?" Fred turned his steed in beside the lieutenant's.

"I don't know of any regulation against it," the lieutenant said. "Only it's pretty tough for a civilian. There's always the chance you'll end up with an enemy bullet in your back. The Apaches aren't likely to know the difference between you and us."

"I'll take my chances," Fred promised.

He stayed several weeks with the outfit, eating with them and sleeping on the ground as they did. He learned that when you are chasing Indians in their own territory, pitching camp is a simple matter. You simply dismount, unsaddle your horse, and the camp is made—no roaring fires, since that would mark your position to the enemy; no trumpets to waken you in the morning for the same reason—only the routine order, "Catch your horse."

Fred learned other things about scouting Indians: you don't unsaddle sweating horses in a broiling sun—it will make their

77

backs sore; nor do you ride along the skyline of a hill exposing yourself like the Statue of Liberty; only an ignorant fool uses a spur if a horse is weakening on a long march. He found out, too, that on the desert, canteen water wets but does not cool.

Sometimes the Indian scouts pointed out drops of blood as evidence that unseen riders had urged their mounts on by cruel knife thrusts in their sides. The scouts were an invaluable asset to the outfit, for they read every hoofprint and twig as plainly as though they were written messages. They remained uncommunicative as to why they had deserted their own people to work for the white men.

One day these scouts led them to a hostile camp. They were seen, and shots rang out as they approached. The men, Fred among them, dashed for the shelter of the rocks. A slug of lead hit an overhanging boulder and bits of rocks poured over Fred and the soldier next to him. The soldier's rifle roared its reply, and Fred, though it was not in his agreement with the lieutenant, drew out his six-shooter. Thus his childhood dream was made a reality. Though there was small likelihood of his hitting anybody, he was actually shooting at hostile Indians. It was like a game to him. He couldn't believe there was danger.

The interchange of shots continued for no more than a few minutes. Then there was silence from the Indian encampment.

"Lay low, young man," Fred's companion whispered. "It's a trick. They're waitin' for us to expose ourselves."

"Maybe they've run out of ammunition," Fred suggested.

"Mebbe." The soldier, a seasoned veteran with reddish hair and long, drooping mustache, gave an indifferent shrug. "There's no way of telling. Who can read an Injun's mind?"

Fred, who had already decided he couldn't, didn't reply.

They waited quite a while, and finally the lieutenant shouted an order to attack. As a unit the men rose up from behind the rocks that had protected them and pushed forward, their rifles held ready. Fred was among them. He could have stayed behind and nobody would have said anything, but he didn't want it that way. In a brief, flashing second he reflected that some would surely have to die, and if he were one of them, that was the way it was.

But the Indian camp ahead of them was deserted. The warriors had vanished as silently as falling snow, and only a few glowing embers of their campfire betrayed that they had really existed.

"How do you like Injun fighting?" the lieutenant asked him at evening mess.

"A bit on the frustrating side," Fred confessed with a wry grin.

Some of the men were suspicious of Fred at first; sometimes they made him the butt of their jokes. Gradually they accepted him for what he was. The soldiers were of many nationalities, Irish, German, Polish, and Italian, and had the kind of rugged, seamed faces with irregular features that he liked to draw. They were pleased at his sketches of them, begging him to let them know when they were to appear in the "Eastern magazines." He would not confess that up until then his appearance in such publications was limited to two sketches, both redrawn by better artists. When he finally left them, it was with vows of friendship and a promise to return the following year.

A few days later he was banging at the door of the Halls' house in Kansas City. "Say, Hall, can you give me something to eat?"

His pockets were empty, which was not surprising, but his portfolio was full. The Halls welcomed him as a prodigal son, but now all he could think of was getting back to Missie and New York City, where he could persuade some of the Eastern editors to pay attention to him. How to get there was another question.

Restless and bored one evening, he strolled into a saloon and ordered a drink, having just enough change to pay for it. As he glanced into the mirror above the bar, his attention was caught by a little drama being enacted behind him. At a small table, two men, obviously professional gamblers, were playing poker with a neatly dressed man in a bowler hat, just as obviously a drummer fresh from the East.

Fred turned with his drink and walked casually toward the back of the room, stopping behind one of the gamblers. There was no doubt about it. The poor drummer was going to be taken for every cent he had if something weren't done about it.

"You're new around here, aren't you, stranger?" Fred addressed the drummer.

The man looked up in surprise. "Why, yes I am, sir? How did you know?"

"It's written on your face," said Fred. "My name's Remington. What's yours?" He offered to shake hands.

"Fitzgerald. Berry Fitzgerald." The man gave him a soft and well-manicured hand.

"Glad to meet you, Fitzgerald. I think you should know you're keeping the wrong company." He made no attempt to lower his voice. "You'd better get out of here quick if you expect to keep coach fare to the next town."

"Oh!" The drummer gasped and stood up, realizing what Fred meant. "Of course, you're right. How good of you, sir. I should have had better sense." He turned to his companions. "Goodnight, gentlemen. I believe I shall retire to my room."

"Hey, what do you think you're doing, butting in here?" one of the gamblers growled at Fred. "If you think you can get away with this, I'll . . ."

"You'll what?" Fred was not the same youth who had lost his

80

money to a couple of tricksters two years back. He was carrying his gun and now he pulled it out and held it on the gamblers. "Get behind me, Fitzgerald." He backed out, until they were safely out the door. Then he escorted the nervous traveler to his room.

"Well, I never expected anything like this in a town as modern as Kansas City," he said as he sat down on his bed and wiped the sweat from his forehead with a white and carefully ironed handkerchief. "I don't know how to thank you, Mr. Remington. Would you be offended if I offered you, well, say some money, as a reward for what you saved me tonight." He drew his wallet out.

Fred felt good. The episode had proved him once and for all an oldtimer. He basked in the gratitude and admiration that shone in the Easterner's eyes.

"Money!" He waved his hand in a grand gesture of dismissal. "Out here in this country, stranger, you don't offer people money for doing what they have to do. Never could stand to see a hare being attacked by a couple of bloodhounds." He swaggered toward the door. It was a fine speech but he felt a little sorry he'd made it when he saw the drummer returning his wallet to his pocket.

"Well, I sure appreciate what you've done. I'll never forget it as long as I live."

"Save your thanks, Berry," Fred told him as he left. "Just remember in the future that there are more ways than one to be a sucker. Keep your door bolted tonight and you'll be all right."

He reconstructed the scene in his mind as he strode home in the early autumn chill. Only he imagined the ending differently. He imagined the drummer saying, "Well, since you won't take money, how about being my guest for the trip back to New York?"

The next day when Fred dined with the Halls he told them the whole story, including his regret that he had not accepted the drummer's money.

"Why, Fred, I didn't know you were so dead set on goin' back East," Mr. Hall said mildly. "I'll be glad to lend you the fare."

"I wouldn't dream of it," Fred protested.

Mrs. Hall rose to clear off the supper dishes. "Nonsense," she said. "Missie has waited for you long enough. Don't argue with us, Fred."

In the end he accepted, leaving as a hostage the painting for which Missie had posed. It showed a young Mexican woman offering a drink to an old United States Army Regular, while in the background two Mexicans squatted in front of an adobe house. The title he gave it was, "Gracias, Señorita! May the Apaches Never Get You."

"We're the ones who are in your debt now," commented Mr. Hall when he accepted the gift.

CHAPTER · 7

Missie, fresh and pretty as a rose, met him in Manhattan and they rented a small room in a Brooklyn boardinghouse. The next day Fred went to see J. Henry Harper, the editor of *Harper's Weekly*, who had bought his first sketches. It was Mr. Harper's policy that his door should be open to everyone; Fred walked in unannounced.

He soon found himself telling all about his Western adventures, not excluding the incident of the Eastern drummer and the two gamblers, to which he added the fictional ending that the drummer out of gratitude had paid his fare back to New York. His conscience gave him only the slightest pang for this deviation from the truth. One thing his evenings around campfires with cowboys and prospectors and soldiers had taught him: if a story is worth telling, it's worth improving.

Harper summoned Henry Mills Alden, the art editor of the magazine; together they went over the contents of Fred's portfolio and finally selected one, the result of his tour with the cavalry outfit, called "The Apache War—Indian Scouts on Geronimo's Trail." It appeared in their issue of January 9, 1886, the first to be reproduced unchanged under Fred's own name.

The payment he received was hardly enough to support a wife, and other editors were cold to him.

His Uncle William Remington came down to New York and took him to visit an old friend of Fred's father: the politician Tom Platt, head of the American Express Company. Mr. Platt gave him a job adding up columns of figures. Fred stood it a week and then went to the manager.

"Do you like this sort of work?" Fred asked him.

The manager looked him over coolly. "Of course or I wouldn't be doing it. We all have to begin at the bottom and work our way up, young man."

"Fine," said Fred. "You do it. I'm leaving."

He confessed to Missie that evening, as they ate the meal she had prepared on the gas plate in their room, that he had quit his job.

"Good," she said. "I couldn't have stood being married to a bookkeeper much longer."

He stared at her despairingly. "Missie, what shall I do? I'm a failure as an artist. And I can't stick at any other work."

At that moment she seemed the only one who could give him the answer to what was torturing him.

"You're not a failure, Fred," she said, rising to pour his coffee. "You're a very good artist—much better than most who get in the magazines all the time. Only you're not as good as you could be. In spite of Yale, you're pretty much self-taught, and there are some things you haven't mastered yet. You don't know enough about perspective and you pay more attention to detail than to your drawings as a whole, which offends some people. I think you should go to a really good school for a while and work at it."

"Why, you're absolutely right," he said wonderingly. "How do you know so much?"

She laughed. "I studied a little while you were gone. After all, the wife of a famous man shouldn't be stupid."

"What school could teach me anything?"

"I've looked into that too," she informed him. "I think the Art Students League on Twenty-third Street in Manhattan would be the best place. The school has been going about ten years— long enough to know what they're doing yet not old enough to be stuffy."

"We'd have to borrow more money if I did that," he said slowly.

She shrugged. "So we'll borrow more money. It will all be paid back one day, never fear."

Again Uncle William came to the rescue with a loan, and the Art Students League turned out to be as helpful to Fred as Missie had anticipated. Unlike the Professor at the Yale Art School, the League instructors did not expect all the students to emulate the Greeks and Romans, but encouraged them to develop their own style and individuality. Fred found it stimulating, too, to exchange ideas with the other students. While he usually disagreed violently with them, at least he had an opportunity to formulate his own theory—which was simply that American artists should stick to America for their training, subject matter, and inspiration.

In a few months Fred felt that the League had taught him everything it could. He was fed up with the city and anxious to keep his promise to rejoin his friends in the cavalry outfit. It meant borrowing more money—their debts were really beginning to look staggering—and again Missie offered no objections but arranged to spend the summer with her parents. Before he left he went back to Alden at *Harper's*. Alden didn't give him any definite assignment, but he did say that they would want to see everything he drew about the Southwest and the Apaches, and that there was a good chance of their buying some of his art work.

June of 1886 found Fred once more in Arizona.

There has been several developments in the Apache War in the last months. Twice Geronimo had offered to surrender, but he was still at large! His first offer was made to Captain Emmet Crawford through a squaw. Geronimo, she said, wanted to talk peace with the captain. But the conference never took place. The next morning some Mexican soldiers met up with Crawford's Indian scouts and mistaking them for Geronimo's hostiles, had fired. Crawford rode in between the two forces, shouting, "Don't shoot." As he did so, a rifle cracked and he was killed instantly.

It was feared in army circles that this would make Geronimo change his mind about surrendering, for Crawford was the one man he had trusted; but he later agreed to meet with General George Crook, who was then in charge of all operations against the Apaches. They met on March 25, 1886, when Geronimo formally agreed to surrender. But that night an American sold whisky to the Indians in direct violation of military rules. By the time Crook heard what had happened, the Indians were crazed with drink and would not listen to him. Geronimo and some twenty of his warriors deserted camp, returning to the Sierre Madres, and the war was on again.

General Crook had an argument with army officials in Washington about their method of treating Indians, and resigned his command. On April 2 General Nelson Miles was ordered to relieve him, establishing his headquarters at Fort Bowie by Apache Pass. General Miles was determined to end the Apache wars once and for all, and stationed troops on both sides of the Mexican border.

Fred had received a note from his lieutenant friend postmarked *Frontares*—a small Mexican town near the border—and it was there he headed, only to find that the lieutenant had departed. He met up with a soldier he had known the previous year, a burly Irish private named Kelly, who elected to become his guide.

"Sure and begorry, you missed a fine funeral, my boy," he said as they stood before an adobe wall at the edge of town. "It was here three weeks back we buried Captain Hatfield's men. By the light of a torch it was, and only a few Mexicans and ourselves as mourners."

He gave Fred the details. On May 15 Captain Hatfield of the Fourth Cavalry had been ordered from his position on the boundary to follow the trail of the hostiles northward. He struck it with the help of a scout, picturesquely named Johnnie Few Clothes, caught up with the Indians and captured their horses and saddles. The Indians had their revenge a few days later; they surprised Captain Hatfield's outfit in a box canyon, stampeding their horses and killing four men. The rest had repulsed the Indians and recovered the bodies of their comrades, which they took to Frontares for burial.

"Why do I always miss out on the big events?" Fred lamented.

"If you hadn't, you might not have that fine head on your shoulders," Kelly commented philosophically.

Kelly's story contained all the elements that Fred liked most —drama, soldiers, Mexicans, and of course, the imminence of death. He finished a drawing of the incident in his hotel and sent it to *Harper's* with the note that it was made "on the spot." It didn't occur to him that this might be misleading. He hadn't after all claimed to be an eyewitness.

Everything about the cavalry interested him; not the least of it was that the men seemed grateful to the Eastern artist who concerned himself with their hard, dull lives. Fred wanted to find another outfit to stay with, but was advised that since General Miles was now in charge, it would be better to get permission from him.

Fred considered this a nuisance. He imagined the general, whom he had missed on his first trip to Miles City, in full-dress uniform, complete with gold braid, seated in style behind his desk and listening to Fred's story with a shade of contempt.

He headed northward to Fort Bowie where Miles had his headquarters. At the fort he made his request to the sentinel at the gate, who summoned the guard, who in turn relayed the message to the general's orderly. This young man informed Fred that the general was not available at the moment; he was out hunting!

Fred waited, chatting with the sentinel and the orderly.

"There he comes," announced the sentinel about a half-hour later as a man mounted on a blue roan galloped toward them.

Fred saw a tall, spare, suntanned person with grizzled hair and mustache. He wore a dusty uniform with trousers rein-forced by buckskin—epaulets and gold braid conspicuously missing. His boots did not shine and as he dismounted Fred noticed that one spur was missing. A half-dozen or so wild turkeys were tied to his saddle horn.

"I didn't do so badly, eh?" the general said with a chuckle to his orderly. "Here take these fowl to the cook."

"Excellent, sir," said the orderly, and presented Fred.

"Glad to meet you, young man." The general offered his hand.

As the orderly, holding the turkeys by their legs, departed in the direction of the mess, the general led Fred inside his barracks to sit by a table in a sparsely furnished room.

"Now tell me what I can do for you," he said as soon as they were seated.

Fred told him, stressing the lack of information in the East as to what the army was doing in terms of day-by-day hardship and routine as well as during moments of the doubtful glamour of battle.

The general listened until he had finished, his face impassive. Then he asked a few questions. How old was Fred? Where in the States did he come from? Where had he gone to school? Had he ever thought of joining the army himself? What had he been doing for the last three years? When Fred had given his answers, he felt that Miles knew him as well as he knew himself.

"What kind of drawings do you do?" The General asked finally.

"I do sketches of men and horses, sir," Fred told him. "I also like to make pictures that tell a story—not a great event necessarily, but something dramatic."

General Miles puffed on his pipe thoughtfully. "For instance, some of my men pushed a batch of Apaches back into Mexico, where they took a stand. Our soldiers made a brave fight, but the enemy knew the land better than we. One soldier, Corporal Scott, was so severely wounded he could not move and was caught in between the two forces, shot at from both directions. As he lay on the ground, one of my officers, Lieutenant Powhatan H. Clarke, a gallant young fellow fresh from West Point, dashed forward and rescued Scott at the risk of his own life. Tell me, Remington, is that the sort of thing you like?"

88

Fred leaned forward eagerly. "It is exactly, sir."

"Well, I tell you what. Tomorrow you ride over to the San Carlos Reservation with me. You ought to see it anyway, and Clarke is over there and you can get the rest of the story from him. How will that be?"

Fred jumped at the chance. "It will be great, sir."

The next morning as he and the orderly galloped along the mountain trails trying to keep up with the general, Fred wondered vaguely if he hadn't made a mistake in coming along. General Miles had learned riding from the Indians, and Indians go uphill and downhill as a matter of course at whatever speed they happen to be traveling. Fred was considerably younger than Miles, but even so matching his pace left him panting and puffing.

At San Carlos the general had business with a member of the Interior Department from Washington. He instructed a captain stationed there to take charge of Fred and left him on his own.

The San Carlos Reservation was a dreary post in the desert next to the Gila River, where the water tasted of alkali, the soil was poor, and flies were a constant plague. Humanitarians pointed out the cruelty of forcing the Apaches to stay in such an unfertile, desolate spot. Practical military men believed that as long as Indians had to choose between the living death of San Carlos and the freedom of their native forests, there would be trouble. Fred was not concerned with the "Indian problem" as such. The visit to him was a marvelous opportunity to sketch. He told his plans to the captain next morning as they were getting ready for breakfast. The man stopped brushing his hair and turned to Fred with a humorous twinkle in his eyes.

"Young man, if you want to live to wear a long gray beard, you'd better not let the people here see you trying to immortalize them on paper."

Remembering his disastrous experience trying to sketch the

Blackfeet on his first Montana trip, Fred promised to be discreet. It was the day that rations were being distributed and squaws crowded around to receive the great chunks of beef that a native butcher threw at them, while groups of old women sat on the sand and gossiped and Yuma bucks galloped past with their long hair flying out behind. Indian scouts in military coats and armed with rifles stood about to preserve order, and young girls with queer ornaments in their hair flitted around. For the most part Fred was ignored. When some of them got suspicious that this young man was trying to steal their images, they vanished like quail.

Before they left, General Miles arranged for Fred to meet Lieutenant Powhatan Clarke, a handsome young officer whom Fred liked immediately.

He explained to the officer that he wanted to know more about his rescue of Corporal Scott.

"My rescue?" the lieutenant repeated blankly. "Did General Miles say I rescued Scott?"

"Yes, he did. He was very definite about it."

Clarke burst out laughing. "I'll tell you something, Remington. It's a weakness of generals that they always attribute heroic actions to the officer in charge. The man who rescued Scott was not myself but a Negro officer named Cloud. My troopers will vouch for it."

Fred still did the picture. He called it "Soldiering in the Southwest: The Rescue of Corporal Scott." But as Clarke insisted, he gave the credit to Lieutenant Cloud. It appeared in *Harper's Weekly* in the August 21, 1886, issue.

Fred left the reservation with the best collection of Indian pictures he had yet done, and also with General Miles' permission to visit any of the military posts of the West he wished to see.

Back in New York, he found that *Harper's* had published several more of his pictures and were buying a couple of others, including the one made "on the spot" entitled "The Burial of Hatfield's Men." This was fine prestige for a beginning artist, but it still didn't mean a living wage. He and Missie took up residence again in Brooklyn, and, portfolio under his arm, Fred started making the rounds of the other big magazines.

They just weren't interested. The editors, mostly genteel, proper little men, seemed shocked and offended by Fred's lusty cowboys and rough, unshaven soldiers. One publisher told him frankly that it was the policy of his magazine to portray America as a growing industrialized country, and that Fred's pictures of a Wild West where Indians still roamed would give the wrong impression—"particularly to foreign powers who are considering investing their money here."

Another criticized him for showing running horses with their legs doubled under them like a crab. "Everyone knows that when horses run their legs are stretched out."

Fred froze. "Do they? Have you ever looked at a running horse—closely?"

"Well, of course," said the editor. "I mean . . ."

"You mean you've looked at them without seeing them," Fred said icily and stalked out.

He met with this criticism frequently, and at first there was nothing he could do about it except become indignant. No one would believe that he saw things ordinary people missed. But about this time Professor Edward Muybridge was experimenting with instantaneous photography, in which he demonstrated the true movements of animals, particularly galloping horses. These showed beyond a shadow of a doubt that they ran with their hoofs folded up under them, as Fred portrayed them.

In the meantime he fought off discouragement and turned his attention to the smaller, lesser-known publications. By chance he wandered into the offices of a sporting magazine called *Outing*. The editor, busy at his desk, hardly raised his eyes high enough to catch sight of Fred's portfolio.

"All right, let's see what you've got." He reached out for it, his voice implying that artists with their wares had been on his neck all day long. He started to go through the sketches rapidly, then slowed down, studied each one separately and nodding thoughtfully.

"I think you've got the real thing here. Good," he muttered, half to himself.

It seemed to Fred that there was something familiar about the man as he noted the humorous lines around his eyes, his brown wavy hair, the smooth, intelligent forehead.

"So your name is Remington," the young editor commented, his gaze still on the sketches. "Not a common name. An odd coincidence—I had a classmate at Yale . . ."

Then it came to Fred. "Big, is that you?" he boomed out.

A moment later the two men were slapping each other on the shoulder with resounding thumps, both talking at once.

"Well, I never . . . Fred, you old so-and-so, it's good to see you."

Finally they settled down to business. "I'm buying every picture you have," Poultney Bigelow informed him. "And not because you're a friend but because they're good."

"You're almost alone in that opinion," Fred confessed.

Big was undisturbed. "Of course I am. They're rough. But that's what is good about them. These so-called art editors here wouldn't stand for an ungroomed horse or a soldier in shirt sleeves. But you'll see. You're going to be famous. I'm going to give you so many commissions you won't be able to come out from under for three years."

Before Fred left the office he was given cash payment for the contents of his portfolio and an assignment to illustrate a series

92

of articles written by Lieutenant John Bigelow called "After Geronimo." When that was settled they went out to lunch.

"Tell me everything you've done since I've seen you," Big ordered.

With little encouragement, Fred launched into his story, skipping over the dreary parts, emphasizing and exaggerating from habit by now, the excitement and the drama. His comparatively small sheep ranch in Butler County turned into a vast hacienda on the Mexican border which he had lost when a fatal disease had struck the sheep. Exaggeration or no, his stories delighted his former classmate.

"One thing is sure," he chuckled delightedly. "Where the Yale Art School failed, the Rio Grande has succeeded. Maybe the Faun of Praxiteles was not for you, but the Apache redskins certainly are."

When Fred got back to Brooklyn that night, he gathered Missie into his arms and swept her off the floor. "Put whatever you have on that gas plate in the garbage," he told her. "We're going out to dinner to celebrate and order the biggest slice of cow this side of the Mississippi. And we're going in a hansom cab."

CHAPTER · 8

Ten issues of *Harper's Weekly* in 1886 carried Frederic Remington illustrations, mostly full-page pictures, several on the front cover with explanatory notes in the editorial section. The October 9 issue carried his first cowboy picture, "In from the Night Herd." He did his first book illustrations that year:

two drawings for Solomon Buckley Griffin's *Mexico of Today*, and he illustrated a serial in the children's magazine *St. Nicholas* called "Juan and Juanita." In *Outing* magazine his illustrations for "After Geronimo" began with the December, 1886, issue. He appeared regularly in that magazine afterward, and in May of 1887 they ran a story which he wrote as well as illustrated on his rabbit-coursing experiences in Kansas.

Lady Success, after having given him the cold shoulder for what had seemed a very long time, was at last beginning to smile on him.

The New York art world gave him token recognition when his "Flag of Truce in the Indian Wars" was hung in the 1887 Annual Exhibition of the American Water Color Society, and "The Courier's Nap on the Trail" was hung in the Annual Exhibition of the National Academy of Design. The next year the National Academy hung his "Return of a Blackfeet War Party," which won both the Hallgarten and the Clarke prizes; while the Water Color Society exhibited his "Arrest of a Blackfoot Murderer by Canadian Mounted Police," based on a sketch he had made on his first trip West.

His illustrations in *Outing* brought him fan mail from all over the country. They also aroused the enthusiasm of a young politician who had graduated from Harvard the same year Fred had left Yale—Theodore Roosevelt. "Teddy" was so excited about Fred's pictures that he persuaded *Century* magazine to let him illustrate his series of articles on "Ranch Life and the Far West," about the large cattle ranch he had been running while Fred had been experimenting with sheep.

Richard Watson Gilder, editor of *Century*, asked Fred to stop in his office. Gilder was an Easterner through and through, born in Bordentown, New Jersey, with considerable reputation as a poet. But he was also a Civil War veteran, knew something about horses, and was attracted by Fred's realistic portrayal of them.

"Tell me about the West," he opened the conversation as he passed Fred a box of cigars.

Fred needed no urging to talk on this subject. The West was the endless prairies of Texas, he said. It was the alkaline stretches of Death Valley, the winter storms of the Dakota Badlands. It was the gray plains of Kansas, the cactus deserts of Arizona, the fragrant pine forests and the snowy peaks of the Rockies, and the frontier towns of Montana. It was vast herds of bison thundering across the plains and the lone timber wolf following its prey. It was the rapids of the Colorado River and the blue depth of a mountain lake. It was Cheyennes and Sioux and Blackfeet and Apaches. And it was French explorers, fur traders with bark canoes, priests in cassocks, buckskin-clad scouts, sunburned cavalrymen, prospectors with burros, rollicking cowboys, pioneers with creaking covered wagons, and settlers with their sod breakers and barbed wire . . . It was the past holding over into the present just long enough for him to get it all down . . .

To all of this Gilder listened attentively. "Now tell me about the Western horse. How does it differ from the Eastern species?"

"The Western horse?" Fred exploded. "There ain't no such critter." There were as many kinds of horses in the West as there were people, he continued, waving his cigar. Some of them stubborn, some gentle, some plain ornery. Of course, though horses had as many "kinks" in their nature as humans, there were certain general types. Take the Texas pony, for instance. Even a man ignorant as sin about horseflesh wouldn't have to walk twice around a Texas pony to know it for what it was— long body, legs fine as a deer's, frequently a pinto hide, small and shriveled up because of the dry, hot climate, and hard as the devil to break.

Or the Canadian Northwest pony: "He's small and scraggy with front feet which will paw through the snow halfway to

China to get at the dry herbage. You'd think he couldn't live ten days, but by hook or crook he lasts the winter through . . .

"The Cherokee pony—you'll find him in Indian Territory, in Arkansas and Missouri—is a peculiar animal. Low stature, generally bald, with thick mane and tail. They say he's derived from Eastern origin, though he's adapted himself to his surroundings. A real handsome little beast."

Or take Indian ponies, he went on. It was a mistake to expect them to have the arched neck, the graceful line of the English hunter. In the typical Indian pony, head and neck joined like two parts of hammer; the belly was huge because of the bushels of grass he consumed. "The Injun doesn't go in for grooming like the white man does, but he will deck out a horse splendidly. I saw a Blackfoot war pony once fitted out with red flannel, brass-headed tacks, silver plates, and feathers. It was enough to take your breath away . . ." He paused. "What else can I tell you?"

Gilder's eyes twinkled as he laid down his cigar. "Well, I see you know the horse. Now what I called you in for was to suggest that you go out West and do some original drawings for us."

To go out West and draw—and be paid for it at the same time, with credentials from a leading New York magazine—it was what Fred had dreamed of. "Sure I'll go," he said offhandedly. "Why don't you send a literary man with me? Someone who could write down the stories I draw."

"Why don't you write them yourself?" the editor suggested unexpectedly.

"The best writing I've ever done was to sign my name on the back of a railroad pass," Fred said, modestly forgetting to mention his humorous article in *Outing* the year before.

"If you can write as well as you talk about the West, you'll have no trouble," Mr. Gilder commented drily.

It was the beginning of a supplementary career for him as a writer, but at the time Fred didn't take it too seriously.

Missie went back to Gloversville for the summer, and June of 1888 found Fred once more in the region of the Pinal Mountains, scouting with the Tenth United States Cavalry, not as a tolerated observer but as an accredited magazine correspondent. In spite of the hard work the last two years he had gained considerable weight since his last visit. He suffered in the long march across the Gila Valley, where even the canteen water was somewhat near the boiling point; the climbs into the rarefied atmosphere of the mountain ranges left him puffing like a tugboat.

He visited the San Carlos Reservation again, where there were still thousands of Apaches and where the agency was now guarded by Negro soldiers. A Chinese ran the officers' mess. "Four races of people in one group," he wrote to Missie. "Quite a commentary on America."

The year 1888 was his biggest yet. He had fifty-four pictures in *Harper's Weekly*, thirty-two in *Outing*, twenty-seven in *Youth's Companion*, sixty-four for the Roosevelt series in *Century*—an incredible output for one man. He worked fast but he didn't lower his standards. Once Big criticized the proportions of a deer in one of the *Outing* drawings. Before he could stop him, Fred had torn the drawing in two. He preferred to do it over rather than to fix it up.

His first illustrated article for *Century* was "Horses of the Plains," which appeared in January, 1889. He slaved over it, reading books and articles on the history of horses since they were brought to the Americas by the Spaniards, to which he added what he learned from observation and from talking to his Western friends.

"Richard Gilder said I knew the horse," he told Big proudly.

"I liked that. When I die I want them to put on my tombstone, *He knew the horse.* Just like that."

"That's not quite all you know," his friend said.

Three other articles, also illustrated, appeared in *Century* in the same year, one called "On the Indian Reservations," describing his first visit to San Carlos.

Debts paid up, the Remingtons considered moving to better quarters. Their choice was an apartment in the Marlborough Tenements, located close to Central Park, where Fred could ride city horses when he felt the urge. The Marlborough, though far from elegant, was a place where they could entertain their friends and where Fred had space to work and to display his now-substantial collection of Western paraphernalia.

He still didn't like formal social gatherings. Some of his Canton friends held a party at a fashionable New York hotel and he couldn't refuse to go. He got his revenge by sending in a card by the headwaiter which read, *The Duke of Marlborough.* For the entire evening the guests fawned on this big, ruddy, blond-haired man who was allegedly a member of the English aristocracy.

He chuckled over it with Missie later that night.

"The funny part of it is that I am supposed to have some blue blood somewhere. According to what my Grandfather Remington used to tell me, the family here is directly descended from a Lady and Lord Thomas Remington, who had an estate of some five thousand acres in York, England. Can you beat that?"

"Why didn't you ever mention your famous ancestors before?" Missie asked.

"What's the difference?" he demanded. "We live in America now. Titles don't mean anything here, thank goodness."

The Marlborough Tenements were soon too small for them, and they moved to a two-family house on Mott Avenue near

138th Street. Fred wrote letters to his friends, telling them that there was no latch on the door and that the pantry was always full of pie.

One man who accepted his widely scattered invitations was Lieutenant Powhatan Clarke, General Miles' protégé. He was a handsome and charming guest, whose narrow waist made Fred conscious of his own increasing girth. Missie, as usual, served them refreshments and then retired discreetly into the background, letting Fred do the talking. When she had gone out to the kitchen for a few moments, the young lieutenant turned to Fred.

"Congratulations," he said.

"For what?"

"For being married to the most delightful young woman I've ever met here or abroad."

"She is?" Fred asked blankly. After four years of married life he had begun to take Missie for granted.

Clarke kept in touch with the Remingtons for years after that, when he was stationed in Germany and later when he bought a ranch in California. But he wrote to Missie as often as he did to Fred, who suspected that Clarke was secretly in love with her.

It was Fred's plan to work through the winters in New York but to return West each summer to gather new material, a plan which Missie agreed would be the best thing for his professional career. He made one such trip down into Mexico in the summer of 1889, among other reasons to make sketches for a serial called "The Aztec Treasure House" by Thomas Janvier, which he had promised to illustrate for *Harper's Weekly.*

In the summer of 1890 he made a brief trip only, returning to spend the rest of the summer at Cranberry Lake in the Adirondacks. He had received an assignment to illustrate Longfellow's *The Song of Hiawatha* in a special edition being put out by Houghton Mifflin. It seemed to him that the green Eastern woodlands and lake country were more appropriate than the Western Rockies for Longfellow's tale.

It was a pleasant interlude. Some days Fred took out one of the Adirondack guide boats, accompanied by a little girl or boy from one of the nearby lodges. His sketching board lay across the gunwales before him, while he drifted around, letting the drawings that did not satisfy him float on the water until they became waterlogged and sank.

At other times he sat out on the little hotel veranda facing the lake, sketching at his easel, his gun at his side. Cranberry was infested with loons that season; every time he spied one he took a shot at it. His overflow of sketches he left scattered on the floor, and sometimes guests picked them up and kept them, either because they liked them or because they guessed their potential value.

Fred liked Cranberry for a variety of reasons, including the fact that the hotel food was good and plentiful and the lake offered the best speckled trout in the vicinity.

In his Hiawatha illustrations for the first and only time in his life he cultivated a romantic idealized style. The Indians were not designated as members of a specific tribe, but were a symbol of all American Indians—of the West, of the East, of the Plains, and of the Mountains—so that they would be suitable for the romantic tone of Longfellow's poem. As compensation he made dozens of small sketches for the margins, which were exact reproductions of items in his collection—moccasins, pottery, papoose baskets, tomahawks and other weapons, war bonnets. In all he did nearly four hundred illustrations.

The new edition of *Hiawatha* was a tremendous success. The name of Frederic Remington became a household word throughout America. Many critics still consider those drawings the most creative, the most purely artistic, he ever did.

When he had finished he went back to join Missie in Canton and spent a few days visiting relatives and old friends.

"You know people think we look rather funny walking down the street together," Missie remarked one evening. "You so big and me so small; you walking on ahead and me trotting behind you like a squaw."

"Do I do that?" Fred asked in amazement. He hadn't realized how he had changed since he had hovered over Missie in the days of their courtship.

He couldn't help bragging to his old pals about his ability to ride wild horses.

"You'll have a chance to show us," one of them said. "There's a circus in town. I'm sure they'd let you have a bronco for a demonstration."

The horse was housed in a livery stable back of the American House facing the village common, and his friends had him ready when Fred arrived the next morning, clad in a new white duck suit, since he considered it an affectation to wear Western clothes in the East. He had just managed to get into the saddle when the bronco took off across the street and into the common. Then it bucked and Fred found himself sailing over his head. His white trousers had taken on a grass-green shade where he landed, and when he limped up to the American House veranda, his comrades were rolling on the floor.

"Well, boys," Fred said amiably. "I guess you'd better set the drinks up on me this time."

Then he and Missie went on to Ogdensburg to visit his mother.

"I have some news for you, Fred," she told him. "I'm going to be married."

"What sort of joke is this?" he demanded.

"It's no joke," she assured him. "His name is Mr. Levis and he's a very nice gentlemen. He is proprietor of the Hodskin

House here in Ogdensburg, and after we're married we're going to run a hotel in Carthage, New York. I think we'll call it the Levis House."

"I won't have it," Fred stormed. "You have no right even to consider such a thing."

"You have no right to tell me what I should or should not do," she said firmly. "You've never paid any attention to what I told you to do. Now I'm going to do what I want."

Fred had to admit that she had logic and reason on her side.

The profits from *Hiawatha* made it possible for him to realize a dream long in the back of his mind—a house of his own somewhere outside the city limits where there were still trees and running water to be seen. He found what he wanted in New Rochelle, in Westchester County, and told his wife about it.

"It's a right big house, Missie, with a gabled roof, an enormous porch, and about three hundred feet of grass lawn in front of it. It's on the crest of the hill and you can look out and see the town and Long Island Sound. There's an old workroom under the roof where I can keep my Western stuff. I'm going to build a wing that I'll turn into the finest studio East or West of the Mississippi." He added: "There's a stable in the back for our horses."

Missie looked up from her sewing. "Are you sure this isn't something you've dreamed up?"

"I'll prove it to you. We'll drive up there tomorrow."

It was true—gabled roof and all. Missie was delighted. "But Fred, it's so huge. You and I will rattle around here like two peas in an empty saucepan."

"Not when I get all my gear in here, we won't," he assured her.

They moved in after all the details of deeds and papers were under control, and Fred drew up plans for his studio. It was to

102

be twenty feet high, forty feet long, and twenty feet wide, with a gigantic fireplace, and double doors wide and high enough so that a mounted horseman could ride in and out if he chose to do so. Fred intended to spend the winter getting everything fixed up.

Instead, the late fall of 1890 found him out in the isolated territory of the Dakotas. The reason for this was a letter he had received from his friend, General Miles.

CHAPTER · *9*

For many years there had been discord between white man and Sioux in the territory of the Dakotas. The government had given the Black Hills to the Sioux, a rich country where they could still live by fishing and hunting. Unfortunately for the Indians, gold has been discovered in these hills, and hordes of prospectors swarmed in, ignoring the terms of the government treaty.

In 1889 a new act of the government cut the Sioux reservation in half, taking away their best hunting grounds. Then Congress announced that their beef rations were to be drastically reduced. The Sioux, faced with starvation, turned to a strange new religion that had been started by an Eastern Indian named Wovoka. Wovoka claimed that he had seen God and that God had told him Indians must live at peace with the white men and put away all thoughts of war. This Ghost Dance Religion, as it was called, spread to other tribes before it finally reached the Sioux and their leader, Sitting Bull.

Although the substance of this religion was peace, white men claimed that it was a religion of war. The agent in charge of the Pine Ridge Reservation in the Dakotas, for instance, became worried and sent telegrams to Washington asking for troops, insisting that the Sioux were planning an uprising. General Miles was put in charge of operations there. It was then that Fred received a note from him, suggesting that if he was still interested in seeing Western troops in action, he should come out. It might be his last chance.

A second lieutenant named Alvin H. Sydenham of the Eighth United States Cavalry made an entry in his journal on the date of October 31, 1890, stating that on that day he met the artist Remington on the dusty alkaline banks of the Tongue River, in the company of General Miles and the Indian Commissioner. He described Fred as a "goodnatured, smoothfaced, fat, blond, original good fellow." He wore, Sydenham went on to say, a little soft hat rolled up at the edges, a brown canvas hunting coat, the swelling pockets of which gave him a downward slope like a brown umbrella. In contrast to the sloppiness of the coat were closely fitting black riding breeches of Bedford cord, reinforced with dressed kid, shapely riding boots, long-shanked English spurs. His face behind the cigar, the lieutenant commented, was fair, blue-eyed, and that of an overgrown boy.

They were introduced. "Sorry to meet you, Mr. Sydenham," Fred said. "I don't like second lieutenants. Never did. Captains are my style of people. They lend me horses." It was a long time since the wide-eyed youth of twenty-four had looked at cavalrymen with awe and taken their ribbing as best he could. Now he was able to give it as well as take it.

"How was your trip, Mr. Remington?" Sydenham asked.

"They say infantrymen can't keep up with cavalrymen, but General Miles is an infantryman and came to camp half an hour ahead of the cavalry troops."

Which was a very mild comment on the journey from Fort

Keogh to the Pine Ridge Agency, which Fred later wrote up for *Harper's Weekly* under the title, "Chasing a Major-General." General Miles, who was fifty-one at the time, "a grim old fellow" in Fred's language, had led them in a mad race, making the two hundred and forty-eight miles between those posts in just thirty-six hours!

Sydenham also noted that, in spite of his weight, Remington rode easily in the saddle and understood and loved horses. When he mounted he patted his mare on the flank, commenting, "I know the shape of every muscle in her body."

Fred hung around the various army posts for nearly two months that cold winter, passing the time on hunting excursions. Finally on Christmas Day, General Miles arranged for him to join the Cheyenne Scout Corps, headed by Lieutenant E. W. Casey. Fred already knew Casey, and admired him as one of the best of the scout officers. He knew some of the scouts too —Wolf Voice with the magnificent physique of an ancient god and the poise of a High Church bishop, and his companions, High-Walking and Stump-Horn.

They camped the first night in the foothills near the town of Hermosa. The Sibley tents were soon pitched, but someone had slipped up and forgotten the Sibley stoves. In the sub-zero temperature they stood around shivering, their only comfort a small holiday toast. After a long and uncomfortable night on the hard-frozen ground, they rose early to breakfast on bacon, "those accursed cracks which are made to withstand fire, water, and weevil," and "a quart of coffee blacker than evil." Then the Sibley tents were rolled up, saddles were adjusted; the Cheyennes mounted their scrawny little ponies, Fred got on the strawberry roan General Miles had provided for him, and the party was off.

Fred had sympathized with the soldiers on summer treks; but that was child's play compared to winter traveling. The scouts, resembling Russian Cossacks in their heavy overcoats, had been at it for a month, and at each stop they flopped down in the dust to sleep, while their little ponies, equally exhausted, stood over them with ears down, heads hanging, and eyes shut.

The second night of camp was colder than the first. The next day, as they rode down the river, Fred spied something moving along the dark gray rocks of the yellow hills. "Sioux" he thought with mingled anticipation and nervousness. He was wrong. The moving dots were pickets of other Cheyenne scouts from the Pine Ridge Reservation. Presently they reached the tepees of their camp, where Casey's scouts greeted relatives and friends with whoops of delight. The Pine Ridge Cheyennes had news for them. Some two nights before, they had had a skirmish with a Sioux war party. They still wore their vermilion war paint. It was contagious, for soon Casey's scouts produced similar streaks of bright red across their faces.

The third day the party split and Fred went off with Wolf Voice and five of the Pine Ridge Cheyennes. They had just begun to cross a frozen river when Fred's smooth-shod roan slipped, landed in the icy water, and with a snort leaped to a safe landing.

"Me think you no like it," Wolf Voice commented as Fred emerged, dripping.

"Your conclusion is correct, Wolf Voice," he said.

Stiffly, in his frozen clothes, Fred followed the rest along a trail that led them to the blue ridge of a high mesa. The trail narrowed, threading its way upward along sheer bluffs. This was no place for riding, and they dismounted, leading their horses. Fred still brought up the rear, puffing and panting, his leg muscles aching at the unaccustomed strain. Finally they were on top, looking over a plain blackened by fire, the dry grass still burning.

They mounted their horses and for half an hour rode over

the plateau strewn with dead cattle, lodgepoles, and the rifle pits from which the Sioux had evidently intended to defend this strip of land. Still the Sioux themselves remained invisible. For his collection Fred rescued a stone pipe and a rawhide stirrup.

In the afternoon they joined Lieutenant Casey and the rest of the scouting party.

"There's trouble," he confided as they rode along together. "A couple of our men were fired on this morning. I have orders not to start anything. The Cheyennes can't understand. For them no fighting means no booty, no enemy ponies, nothing. I don't know how much longer I can hold them off."

Fred agreed that it was a difficult problem.

Casey turned in his saddle to look at him. "You want to know something, Remington? I figure you're just as bad as the Cheyennes. You'd like to see a good fight so you can write about it in that Eastern magazine."

"Oh, I wouldn't say that," Fred murmured uncomfortably. The lieutenant had come all too near to hitting the nail on the head.

He and Casey were riding some distance ahead of the scouts when over the hill Fred finally saw them—a horde of Sioux riding down on them.

"Follow me," Casey called to Fred and, turning, galloped back to his men.

He raised his hand to call the Cheyennes to a halt. Then with his hand on his six-shooter he shouted, "I'll shoot the first man through the head who falls out of the ranks!"

The Cheyennes looked sullen but they obeyed. Fred watched in some bewilderment as Casey led them down the hill to the left, where he ordered them to dismount, though not to remove their saddles. Then he galloped, alone, toward the enemy.

Through his field glasses Fred could see him as he approached the Sioux, his right hand raised in the Indian sign of peace. He never knew what Casey said to the Sioux, but they did not attack. When Casey returned, he announced simply that it was time to make camp.

It was arranged that the next day Fred should return to Pine Ridge in the company of an interpreter named Thompson, two scouts, and a Swedish teamster. Casey assured him that they had the word of the Sioux they would not be stopped and the men didn't even take their carbines.

They had gone about ten miles when six young Sioux warriors appeared out of nowhere and informed them, through Thompson, that they must go back! The Sioux were armed. There was no use explaining to them that Lieutenant Casey had extracted a promise for their safe-passage from other Sioux. The teamster turned his wagon around. As they were about to start back, Thompson gave Fred a quick warning look. Fred turned, and found one of the warriors just behind him, holding a knife.

Without stopping to think, he said, "How, *colah*," and held out his hand. *Colah* means "friend." The Indian took his hand, though he didn't seem pleased.

On their way back to camp Fred loitered behind, hoping to get another look at the warriors so he could study their war dress. He was successful, for suddenly they were around him again, savage and menacing.

They made him get off his horse and searched him for weapons, which he did not have. Then they opened his portfolio and pulled out the drawings, passing them around, making gutteral exclamations as they did so. It was impossible to tell whether they were outraged or impressed with his work. Then they let him get on his horse and ride on. But they kept the sketches.*

* Oddly enough, this incident does not appear in Remington's own account of his Sioux experiences, though it is cited in an article about him in the New York *Times* of January 20, 1929.

That night Fred set off once more from Casey's camp for Pine Ridge, in the company of a Captain Baldwin. They reached the agency just as the wounded were being brought in from the most tragic event of the 1890 battle against the Sioux, an event that would go down in history as the Wounded Knee Massacre.

By this time Sitting Bull, the doughty spokesmen for the Sioux, was dead, shot by Indian police in the pay of the whites, on the dubious charge of trying to escape arrest. The attack of the Seventh Cavalry at Wounded Knee on the night of December 29, 1890, was directed against a band of Minneconjoux Sioux headed by the Indian Big Foot. Two hundred and ninety-eight Indians in all were shot down, of which it was later established that two hundred were women and children!

Current news stories discounted the horror. An article in *Harper's Weekly* of February 6, 1891, by a participant, Lieutenant Gresham, exonerated his comrades of guilt by stating that it was difficult for the inexperienced to distinguish between a squaw and a buck. The lieutenant added: ". . . the sharp chastisement at Wounded Knee has had a salutory effect." In history the massacre would remain as a black mark against white man's warfare.

Fred knew none of these statistics when he returned to Pine Ridge, and if he had he likely would have agreed with Lieutenant Gresham. His love of the army was not so idealistic that he thought all the men and the officers were saints. But for him the Army as a whole, as an entity in itself, could do no wrong. Besides, his interest as always was not what the men in Washington said or did, but in the feelings, adventures, sufferings and triumphs of the soldiers themselves.

Like the good reporter that he was, he didn't waste time regretting that he had missed a big fight, but went around from cot to cot in the field hospital, asking, "What was it like? What really happened?"

"Why don't you go ask General Forsyth?" one young officer with a bandage over his nose asked him. "He was in charge."

Fred smiled disarmingly. "The general's report will be in the newspapers. I want to know what really went on. Only you men who were there can tell me that."

"You want to know?" The young man indicated his nose. "Rather close, don't you think?"

"An inch closer would have been too close," Fred agreed solemnly.

"I'll tell you something," another man shouted from his cot. "The way those Sioux worked their Winchesters was beautiful. I have to say it, even if I'm the one that suffered from it."

Soon they were all talking about their experiences as though Fred wasn't there—which was what he wanted. About the way the Indians raised their arms to heaven before they fired—"a plumb crazy thing to do when you think about it." About their strange belief that no bullet could touch them, which the army certainly had disproved. All these snatches of war talk would make this hospital scene real to the people back home.

The three articles Fred wrote later about the Sioux "outbreak" were of little historical value compared to his illustrations—the United States Infantry in winter uniforms; the troopers in their long overcoats; the proud Sioux in feathered headdress throwing up his hands in an act of devotion before he fired; the soldiers in review at Pine Ridge before General Miles after the victory. There was truth in those drawings for anyone who wanted to know what Indian warfare was really like in that winter of 1890-91.

Fred benefitted in other ways from this trip to the Dakotas. The wintry scenes impressed themselves on him, not only because of their beauty but because of the threat of death for traveler and beast. Such paintings as "Last March," which portrays an exhausted horse dragging weary limbs through the snow while hungry wolves dog his steps awaiting his final fall; "The Hungry Winter," which shows a solitary wolf against a background of snow and skeleton trees and Indian tepees in the distance, and many others with death and winter in the atmosphere had their origin in that cruel winter.

The day after Fred watched the triumphal review of soldiers at Pine Ridge to celebrate the end of the last Sioux war, he was eating his breakfast in the dining car of a train headed for New York and Missie. He had a Chicago morning paper before him and unbelievingly he stared at the headlines. *Lieutenant E. W. Casey Shot*, it read. He continued to read, hoping there might be a mistake, but the dispatch left no room for doubt. Casey, whom Fred knew to be a true friend of the Indians, had been killed by one of the very Sioux he had wanted to protect from bloodshed.

His anger and sorrow mounted. He still could not understand that the killing of his friend was an act of revenge, not against one white man but against all those who were directly or indirectly responsible for crimes like the one committed at Wounded Knee.

CHAPTER · *10*

In 1891 Fred was invited to join the exclusive Players Club on New York's Gramercy Park, along with two other famous artists, Childe Hassam and Charles Dana Gibson, and the dramatist Augustus Thomas who was the Remingtons' neighbor in New Rochelle.

When Fred showed up in the dignified lounge of the Club with its imposing twenty-ton stone mantel by Stanford White, he was appropriately dressed—tall silk hat, fashionable dark blue coat, tan kid gloves, patent-leather shoes, stanch walking stick with buckhorn handle. Except for his boyish, smooth-shaven face, it would have been difficult to believe that this portly gentleman was barely thirty years of age. It was equally difficult to believe that he had recently ridden the plains in khaki dress and that he was an expert with the lasso and a six-shooter. When he opened his mouth, however, the impression changed. His speech was still that of the West, filled with terse epigrams and curse words derived from army friends, cowboy comrades, and Spanish *vaqueros*. Adolph, the headwaiter, was perhaps the most impressed of all; never had the Club had a member with such an enormous appetite!

Fred's studio at New Rochelle was finally finished to his liking. The head of a monstrous moose, which he himself had shot, decorated the great fireplace. The walls were covered with his Western trophies—tomahawks, Indian clubs, lances, bows and arrows, guns and cavalry sabers, cowboy whips, skulls of horses and buffaloes, human scalps, knives, pipes, army drums and sticks, buckskins from different Indian tribes. There was even one buckskin costume which he claimed was a personal gift from Calamity Jane.

He called the New Rochelle mansion and the acres around it "Eudion," and there was a story attached to the name. He and a companion were being piloted by a Chippewa guide on a river somewhere in Canada.

"What do you call your home?" Remington asked their guide.

"Tepee," said the Indian.

"I don't mean that. I mean the place where you have your tepee. The place you go when you are idle."

"Oh, the place where I am at." The Chippewa nodded as comprehension reached him. "Him I call *Eudion*."

The named seemed appropriate and Fred adopted it.

112

The big, rambling house called for friends, and there was never a lack of them. Many of them were famous people and this was not because Fred was a snob—he wasn't—but because he gravitated naturally to men who accomplished things. Writers and other artists came there, and so did military men, such as General Miles, General O. O. Howard, and Colonel Leonard Wood. With the exception of Missie's young sister Emma, who stayed with them weeks at a time, there were almost no women guests.

By this time Fred had illustrated more articles than he could remember, and many of the authors of these articles became intimate friends, for instance the writer Julian Ralph, whom he once called the most interesting fellow he ever met; General Randolph Marcy, whose articles on big-game hunting in the Wild West he had illustrated for *Outing*; the novelist Owen Wister; and of course Theodore Roosevelt, who not only considered Fred the best artist of all times but expressed the opinion that he and Owen Wister were the best writers about the West that the country had yet produced.

The Northern American Continent, East and West, North and South, offered Fred everything a man could wish for; and the last thing from his thoughts was that he would ever consider going farther afield. Then one day his old friend, Poultney Bigelow, put a new bee in his bonnet.

Big was no longer with *Outing*, which had gone bankrupt, but was doing free-lance articles for *Harper's Weekly*. He had persuaded them to let him do a European trip, with the main stopover to be Russia. His idea was that he and Fred should take along canoes and paddle down the Volga from Saint Petersburg to the Caspian, a distance of a mere twenty-five hundred miles or so, with Fred making sketches and Big making notes for articles en route. The idea was just fantastic enough to appeal to Fred.

There were weeks of preparations. Though the canoes were ordered from Everson, the fittings were from a Canton man, Henry Rushton, who even when Fred was a youth had a reputation for sturdy boat-making. These canoes had hatches, sleeping quarters, tents, sails, plus a fine mahogany desk that also doubled as an easel. Fred even invented a waterproof holder for his sketching material, exactly fitted to his canoe.

The Hamburg-American Steamship Company allowed them to take the canoes along as part of their personal luggage, a great convenience. From Hamburg the boats would be sent to Lübeck by rail and then by steamboat to Saint Petersburg. Big and Fred were delighted that the entire charges from Hamburg to Saint Petersburg came to only twenty dollars. It was proof indeed they were not as extravagant as their reputation claimed.

Poultney Bigelow sailed first to spend some time in Germany, while Fred remained behind to complete the final arrangements. He felt rather guilty about leaving Missie. She didn't expect or want to go with him on his Western trips, but a trip to Europe was another matter.

He talked her out of it: "It would be too dangerous for you, Missie. You know what Russia is like these days—secret police, Nihilists plotting to bomb the Czar, spies, people disappearing, chain gangs in Siberia."

"In other words," she said, smiling, "it's just your dish of tea."

"Well . . ." admitted Fred doubtfully.

He went first to Paris, staying at the Hotel Continental, and made a note that, although the city was gay and festive, the big trouble was that people didn't talk English—though they talked more than anywhere else he had ever seen. He dutifully visited all the art galleries, but the masterpieces of the Louvre and the other museums failed to impress him.

From there he went to London, where he thought that at least there would be no language problem. He was wrong. All his attempts to ask his way, order food, or engage in casual conversation were met with the same bewildered looks. English as it was spoken out in Arizona, Texas, and Kansas was as good as a foreign language to Britishers.

Finally he joined Big in Germany and they set off through Poland for Russia. At Alexandrowo they took a private compartment on a train headed for Warsaw. Warsaw was in the part of Poland that virtually belonged to Russia, and an intense program of Russification had been taking place, just as in German Poland there was an effort on the part of the Prussians to imbue the Poles with German ideology.

But Fred and Poultney had no cause to worry—or so they thought. Each carried a document labeled *Special Passport*, issued by the United States government, signed by the ex-Secretary of State, James J. Blaine, and dated March 4, 1892. These papers requested that the bearers pass freely "without molestation and be given such friendly aid and protection as would be extended to like citizens of foreign governments resorting to the U.S."

In addition, Poultney had been commissioned by the United States government to make a report upon "ways to protect the seacoast against wind and waves" by noting what was being done on the sandy shores of the Baltic, where conditions were similar to the shores of Long Island and New Jersey.

With such documents they felt themselves perfectly safe.

The door of their compartment opened and a tall, bearded official wearing an Astrakhan hat, loose trousers tucked into long boots, and a tunic belted at the waist, stood before them. He glanced sharply at them, consulted a piece of paper he was holding, then turned and said something to a similarly dressed man just behind him.

Fred and Big looked at each other questioningly.

The officials didn't ask to see their documents, merely took a look at their tickets, and then departed, slamming the door.

"They didn't look like conductors to me," Fred commented when they were gone. "What do you think they wanted?"

"A ruble perhaps," Big said. He rolled up his jacket and, using it as an improvised pillow, stretched out on the wooden bench.

Fred was not ready to dismiss the matter so easily. "The one with the beard had more than a nickel's worth of scowl on him. I'll wager he was comparing you with the photo on his paper. You've grown a beard since your last passport."

There was no answer. If Big wasn't already asleep, he was pretending to be.

At Warsaw they handed their valises to the hotel porter, but instead of taking an omnibus or cab, they slipped out through the crowd, and with the aid of a map strolled about the streets to get their bearings before checking in at their hotel.

Big stopped in front of a large drugstore. "I have to look up a friend," he said. "Come inside with me. We'll pretend we're here to buy toothbrushes."

"What are you up to?" Fred demanded, mystified.

"You'll see. Just follow me and you'll learn how things are done in Poland."

They went inside and studied the limited assortment of toothbrushes. A clerk came up. Big said, *sotto-voce*, that he would like to see Mr. So-and-So.

"Is that the name of your friend?" Fred said out of the side of his mouth as the clerk walked toward the rear of the store. "No."

Another man joined them. Big said he would like to see him alone. They left Fred still eying toothbrushes, and disappeared in a back room. His friend came back alone in about fifteen minutes.

"Now maybe you will tell me what all this is about," Fred said angrily once they were on the street again.

"Whew!" exclaimed Big, pushing back his cap and wiping his forehead with his handkerchief. "I've just heard plenty. We did a smart thing by not going to the hotel first. Otherwise we would have been trailed here. He said we shouldn't try to see Zerowski now—that's the name of my friend—but should go to the hotel to avoid suspicion. He assured me that a police spy would come to our room five minutes after we surrendered our passports and that said spy would pretend to love Americans. He also said that we're not to say anything while a servant is in the room and that our baggage will be searched thoroughly."

"And who is this Zerowski?" Fred demanded, scowling.

"Oh, a Polish patriot I met in Paris. An intelligent sort of chap. I thought if I saw him here he could tell me what was going on. After all, I'm a journalist, you know."

It seemed to Fred, who forgot momentarily about how he had battled Indians with the Cavalry just to get some good pictures, that this was carrying journalism a bit too far. "And when are we to meet this Mr. Zerowski?" he asked with heavy sarcasm.

"At the Café Tomboff at three-fifty this afternoon. Zerowski will join us there, quite by accident, of course."

"You know what I think?" Fred commented. "I think we should go back to Germany. Or Hungary or Turkey or Africa."

In their hotel they were still discussing whether or not they should keep the café appointment when their door opened and a bald-headed, stoutish man of about fifty walked in. "I thought I heard you say 'Come in'." He spoke in English but with a heavy accent.

Fred and Big exchanged glances. Neither had heard a knock. The stranger sat down and started asking questions. Had they

117

just arrived from Berlin? Where did they last stop before reaching Warsaw? Did they have friends in the city? Where were they going next? Would they like a guide? He added that he loved Americans . . .

The two Americans took turns in evading his questions and finally he left.

"He made up my mind for me," Fred announced grimly. "We're going to the Tomboff."

They had no sooner taken seats in the café than the bald-headed man arrived. He took a chair in the far corner next to another sinister-looking but younger character. The bald-headed one talked to him in a low voice with frequent glances at Fred and Poultney, then departed.

"Here comes Zerowski," Big whispered a moment later.

The tall Pole stood at the threshold hesitantly, strolled the length of the room as though looking for a seat, and then stopped in front of their table. "Do you gentlemen mind if I sit down?"

He gave no sign of recognition as he took his place. The waiter brought him coffee. He offered Fred a cigarette, as to a stranger. As he leaned over to light it, he whispered, "We can't talk here. A Secret Service agent is watching us." A wonderful title for a picture, thought Fred. "You will both be my guests at the theater tonight. I will send two tickets by messenger to your hotel. Tell the hotel porter where you are going." He rose, bowed formally, and was gone.

The theater that night was crowded and hot. Fred sat restlessly throughout the first act, unable to understand a word of the dialogue. He spied Zerowski in a seat back of them. They met him in the garden during intermission.

"Thank God the agent is gone," the Pole said. "He saw that we were not together and gave up. Now we can talk freely. There are things I think the Americans should know." He kept his voice low as he went on to say that a large group of university students were being deported for patriotic activities . . . that the Czar had cut Poland off from all intercourse with the rest of Europe . . . that the Polish people were faced with starvation, and that the Russian police controlled schools and newspapers. "My children dare not speak their mother tongue. Even my servants are selected by the police . . . Russia is dragging us into the mud."

He smiled gently as he spoke. An outsider might have thought he was uttering some not-too-damaging criticism of the play.

The next day the travelers were on their way to Saint Petersburg, Fred at least relieved that Big's curiosity had not got them into deeper water. The first thing they did on their arrival was to visit the luxurious United States Legation.

Their business was only routine, something they both expected to be settled in a matter of moments. Big had sent a letter the week before, outlining his seacoast commission and explaining that they had brought cruising canoes to sail down the Volga. To clinch the matter, he had offered to pay the expenses of anyone the Russian government wished to send along as a guide. If the Russian "guide" turned out to be a spy, they figured, they had nothing to hide.

At the Legation they asked the servant to see the American Ambassador. After a long wait a dapper young man appeared. There was no United States Ambassador in Saint Petersburg, he said. He was the first secretary, who acted as attaché. He was, of course, at their service.

Big, whom Fred willingly let act as spokesman, explained that they had come for the permission requested in their letter.

What letter? The attaché asked with raised eyebrows. No such letter had been received.

That came as a shock, but Big rallied to show their special passports and other documents.

The attaché looked them over and returned them. "I'm sorry, gentlemen, but I would say that these lack diplomatic form." He added that the Russian government was resentful of foreigners who came to report upon things in Russia.

Big flushed. "We have the fullest guarantees to prove the innocent nature of our cruise."

The attaché smiled and shook his head. "I'm afraid that you have come on a fool's errand, though of course I will see what I can do."

They took a droshky back to the hotel. It seemed to Fred that everyone they saw on the streets was either in uniform or in rags. "How long do you think it will take that attaché to get action?" he asked. "I don't relish sticking around here too long. Darn it, Big, isn't there one good English sign on a shop window instead of all these hieroglyphics?"

They decided that if the Russian government gave them no answer in the next three days they would take their canoes to the first German port, cruise the Kaiser's coast first, then return to Russia. With Poultney's letters of introduction, time passed pleasantly enough, for high functionaries invited them out, served them champagne and caviar, and promised to do everything possible for their convenience except the one thing they wanted most.

On the third day, when his friend was out, Fred decided to take a drive on his own to the suburbs as a change from city streets. He soon became aware that a second droshky was following him. It passed him, and he saw the occupant speaking to what he took to be a policeman on the road ahead. When his driver reached that point, the policeman ordered him to turn back. He did, depositing Fred at his hotel. Fred's foreign vocabulary, consisting almost exclusively of Spanish curses, got him nowhere. Big returned to find him pacing his room like a caged lion.

"I've had enough," he roared. "Let's get out."

The morning of the fourth day they called at the United States Legation again. The impressive footman told them His Excellency was in bed. They sent a card, asking if there was any news for them. The servant returned with the message that His Excellency had no news, did not know when he would have any, and that there was no use in their waiting.

Poultney, foreseeing that this might happen, had already arranged with the head of customs to have their canoes shipped by fast freight to Kovno on the river Niemen, near the Polish frontier. He had also instructed the hotel porter to have their passports in readiness.

In spite of his foresight, the porter did not have their passports, explaining apologetically that there had been a "little difficulty" at the police station.

They returned to their hotel room. "This is it," Big said gloomily. "Without passports we can't even leave Saint Petersburg. We aren't human beings, we're merely numbers in a police record."

It was Fred's turn now to offer consolation. "They'd better have those passports ready in a hurry or I'll blow the whole town to bits," he exploded.

Big burst out laughing. "You know, Fred, you're the most original and entertaining traveling companion in the world. But you are as perverse as a mule on a railway track, and there are moments when I wonder if you have good sense."

"Have you anything better to suggest?"

"No. Except to wait for a miracle."

"We'll have to make our own miracles to get out of this one," Fred snorted.

Strangely enough, the miracle arrived of its own accord, not ten minutes later, in the form of a Russian prince, a close friend of the Czar's and an aide-de-camp to a grand duke. He had

121

received one of Poultney's letters of introductions and had come to pay them a formal call. He wanted them to visit at any one of his many country places for as long as they liked and was anxious to do anything he could to make their stay a pleasant one. His manner changed visibly when Big urged him to assist in getting back their passports without delay so they could leave.

"There is surely some mistake," he said formally and chatted on about trivial matters while the two Americans inwardly fumed. Abruptly he bowed, excused himself, and out in the corridor they heard a loud altercation.

He returned presently, smiling. "Everything will be all right now," he said.

Within minutes a messenger arrived with their passports.

The next day on the train between Saint Petersburg and Kovno, they ran into another of Poultney's many friends, a man who knew something of the devious ways of the Czar's government.

At first he laughed when they described their misadventures. Then he became grave. "I would advise you to disappear from Russia as soon as possible. You aren't going to get the permission you want."

"And if we take our cruise without permission?" suggested Fred. "I've taken hundreds of cruises in the States and never had to ask permission."

"This is not America," Poultney's friend reminded him. "If you tried it here, the luckiest thing would be that you would be arrested. More likely, some dark night your boats would be smashed to kindling and you would be severely damaged yourselves."

"The Russian government would go to such extremes?" Fred's indignation mounted.

The man shook his head. "Of course not. They would deny vigorously that police agents had any connection with the incident and would blame common thieves."

At Kovno, Fred and Poultney took a steamboat down the Niemen toward the frontier. The boat was full of peasants in colorful costumes and Fred, feeling safe at last, drew out his sketchbook and started to draw what he saw.

An officer sauntered over and made a long speech with many gestures. Fred nodded and smiled, though he understood nothing, and went on working. The officer started all over again, and this time Fred grasped that the man was getting very annoyed about something. He called to Big, who was on the other side of the deck, to come over and do some interpreting. For the third time the officer went through his speech routine, this time in French.

"He says you'd better put away your sketchbook," Big explained. "He says that dire things may happen to you if you don't. He says we must understand that he is offering this advice only as a friend."

Fred glared. "That does it." He rose, closed his sketch pad, and threw it overboard.

"You didn't have to be so hasty," Big protested, too late. "How are you going to illustrate my articles now?"

"You think I'll forget anything I see on this trip?" Fred demanded roughly. "Don't worry, you'll have your picture—provided we can get out of here alive."

"We will," said Big. "That is, if you don't let that officer know you have a camera for a brain."

Until they crossed the frontier the officer kept them under close surveillance.

CHAPTER 11

"We're safe at last," Big said with a sigh as their train carried them away from Russia and into the northeastern corner of Prussia, "though how we escaped arrest I'll never know."

"I'd have torn the whole Russian police force to pieces if they had tried to lay hands on us," Fred announced. "Where to now?"

"We get off at the next stop." That was all Big would say.

Not ten minutes later they quit the train at a small village which he deigned to inform Fred was called Trakehnen. It was a desolate spot and the station was empty. As the two men stood on the platform, travel-worn and weary, their bags beside them, an open carriage drawn by two sleek brown horses pulled up. A driver in uniform leaped down, walked over to them, and saluted sharply.

"Herr Bigelow?" Big nodded and the driver seized their bags. "You are to come with me."

The carriage started off down a beautiful avenue between rows of towering oak trees.

"I hope you know what you're doing," Fred muttered. He half expected they would end up in the prison they had so miraculously missed in Russia. Instead, the carriage took them to a large vine-covered house with a mass of brilliant flowers around the porch. A Prussian officer, with monocle and waxed mustache, came down the path to meet them, his arms outstretched.

"Herr Bigelow! I am enchanted," he said.

Big introduced him: "This is my old friend, Major von Frankenburg. He has kindly offered us his hospitality while we recover from our Russian ordeal. Major, this is the American artist, Frederic Remington."

"Pleased to meet you." Fred shook hands with his usual mighty grasp.

"I am honored," the major told him. "I trust you'll find much inspiration for your work during your stay here."

Well, here at least was one foreigner who didn't think an artist was synonymous with being a spy. Also, he could talk English understandably, albeit with an accent. Fred breathed easier.

After a sumptuous lunch the major suggested that they go for a drive, exchanging glances with Big as he did so; and Fred saw his friend nod slightly. They were up to something, he concluded, but he wouldn't give Big the satisfaction of asking questions.

They were driving along an open country road when abruptly their driver stopped at the edge of a field. And here Fred, who had remained unmoved by the most spectacular scenery that Europe had to offer, gasped in delight.

"Hey, look!" he yelled like a school boy. "Do you see what I see?"

Grazing and cavorting in the field were at least a hundred beautiful young stallions, their coats shining and glistening in the July sun, their movements free and graceful.

Big grinned smugly. "I thought you'd like it, Fred. I should explain that you are now visiting Kaiser Wilhelm's stud farm. The major here is in charge of training horses for the Kaiser and for all the mounted officers of the palace, as well as some hundreds of thousands of mounts for their peacetime army. This is just a sample."

"Say . . . that's splendid!" Fred jumped down from the carriage to get a closer look and the other two men followed.

The horses were beauties, there was no doubt about it. They were being guarded by two mounted herders who had no saddles or stirrups but were sitting upon blankets strapped to their steeds' backs. They carried whips, which they flourished occasionally but only as a warning to keep their herd together. None of the horses seemed in the least disturbed at the approach of the carriage. In fact, they paid no attention whatever to the three men.

Fred saw Big walking right toward the herd. "Come back, old man," he called out. "You'll be trampled to death."

In reply, Big strode straight up to one of the animals, giving him a friendly pat on the flank. The creature didn't budge.

Fred turned to the major. "Get him out of there. He doesn't know what he's doing."

The major tugged at the end of his mustache. "Ah, Mr. Remington, you don't understand. From the time they are colts our horses are trained not to be afraid. A centurion—that is the man in charge of a hundred horses—would be severely punished if one of them shied at a man's approach."

"Well, I'll be . . ." Fred stared in amazement.

Big returned, safe and untrampled. "How'd you like to ride one of these, Fred?"

"I'd like it fine," Fred said. "That is, if the major . . ."

"But of course," Von Frankenburg interrupted. He barked a short command in German to one of the herders, who promptly dismounted, threw a rope around the neck of a beautiful bay, and led him up, securing a saddle produced by the driver from beneath the seat of the carriage. The bay stood docilely while Fred hoisted his mighty bulk up—and then they were off at a long, majestic trot.

For Fred it turned out to be torture. The unaccustomed Eng-

126

lish saddle gave him the feeling he might be propelled out into space at any moment. The bouncing he received seemed to knock all his bones together into one congealed, aching mass. Somehow he managed to keep his seat and his dignity, but once around the field he slid off with great relief.

"Whew," he said, wiping his forehead. "I feel worse than I did when I galloped two hundred miles after General Miles in Arizona hill country."

"It is the trotting," said the major with the utmost gravity. "One must get used to it, of course."

In the following days Fred explored every inch of the Kaiser's stud farm. He watched as the keepers rubbed and brushed and curried each of the young colts every day, stroking them gently and raising each foot in turn, until the colts became accustomed to them and would stand without being tied. He went out into fields where the young horses were divided by color, the blacks in one corner, the browns in another, the bays in the third. If one strayed into the wrong group, he noted with astonishment, the herder simply called him by name and the colt promptly galloped back to his mates of the same color. Much as he admired the discipline and careful training devoted to the horses, at times he felt homesick for the ill-tempered army mounts.

With this pleasure they mixed business, and in the afternoons Big worked on his article for *Harper's* about their Russian adventure, calling on Fred to illustrate it. Could Fred remember, he asked, the farm wagon they had passed on their way down the river, the peasant group on the boat, and the dragoons at the frontier?

Fred promptly sat down with pen and ink and sketched out all three scenes from memory.

"You're like the Japanese artists of the old school," Big said admiringly. "The art master used to take the students for a walk and make them watch the rushes by the lake, or the effect of the breeze on the water, or a flock of cranes flying in formation. Then he would make them draw what they had seen over and over until they had absorbed every movement and every flash of color."

"I don't see the connection," Fred commented as he went on drawing. "I'm not a Japanese artist. I'm an American."

Big did another article while they were staying with the major which he called "Sidelights on the German Soldier." To illustrate it Fred sketched Dragoon and Uhlan officers, a cuirassier, a Guard Hussar, and even a general, using as models the men who visited the stud farm. But while the details of their uniforms and even their facial expressions were all accurate, his reproductions were as stiff and lifeless as toy soldiers. A curious thing about his art, which he freely admitted to himself, was that only when he drew the West could he succeed in breathing life into his subjects.

One day Major von Frankenburg supplied them with a Victoria carriage drawn by two black mares for a trip into the forests of Kaiser Wilhelm's private hunting grounds. It was a wonderful drive along a winding road between towering evergreens and oaks and poplars, past sparkling streams—stocked with trout and perch and carp, the driver informed them over his shoulders—through picturesque little villages that looked as though they belonged on picture postcards, on into the haunts of the wild boar and the big red deer. The latter were easily visible from the roadway and seemed quite unafraid.

"What I wouldn't give to have my Winchester," Fred murmured.

"You can be glad you don't," chuckled Big. "Poaching, even from visitors, is the mortal sin in these parts. Only the Emperor hunts here."

All this tantalizing hunting ground for the benefit of one man? It was an outrage, Fred felt, and he started to say so. A warning glance from Big, accompanied by a gesture directed toward the back of the driver's neck, stopped him. Here as in Russia he had to learn to keep his mouth shut.

Later, with a letter of permission Big had procured from the Lord Chamberlain at Potsdam, they visited Kaiser Wilhelm's newly completed hunting lodge. Fred forget his pique in genuine admiration of the place.

"This is something my size. I wouldn't mind having a place like this myself."

The lodge was a cross between a Swiss chalet and an American log cabin, with massive carved rafters coming to a point in a grinning dragon's head—a feature of Scandinavian architecture, Big said. Wide windows looked down over rustic terraces to the valley below. Opposite them was a great double fireplace. Hunting scenes hung on the walls, which their guide told them had been painted by the Kaiser himself and which Fred considered very poor indeed. He was much more impressed by a collection of huge antlers above the fireplace.

The antlers were all trophies of the Emperor, the guide said with an almost personal pride. The Emperor was an excellent shot. He showed them a rifle with an exceedingly long stock. It was the Emperor's favorite gun for deer hunting, he told them, and showed them how with the long stock the Emperor could use it with his right arm alone—since his left was unfortunately withered and useless.

"Isn't he afraid some of those Muscovite cowboys will traipse across the border after him?" Fred blurted out.

"The Emperor is afraid of nothing," the guide said stiffly after Big had translated Fred's question. "He has only an escort of six police."

Fred knew he was expected to admire the courage and the evidences of good markmanship of the Kaiser, but he couldn't bring himself to do it. A man didn't have to be much of a sportsman to shoot deer in a forest where no one else was allowed to hunt. He longed to proclaim that in democratic America the forests were open to all. But he restrained himself—first, because he didn't want to get them in trouble, and second, because he knew that Big had a soft spot for Kaiser Wilhelm II. Had they not, as boys, played bows and arrows together? To get over an awkward moment he professed himself very thirsty and asked where he could get a drink of water.

They stayed three weeks with the major. During this time Big had been sending telegrams regularly, plus considerable cash, in attempts to retrieve their canoes from the Russian officials. Eventually their boats arrived—with Fred's handsome mahogany desk smashed to pieces. It was hard to fathom why. If the Russians had wanted to see what was beneath the desk, all they had to do was to open the hatches, which were unlocked.

After taking leave of the major, they went to Berlin, where Big arranged to present Fred to the Emperor in person. The pomp and formality of the court didn't appeal to him at all. That Big presented him as *the* most important artist in America, and that the Kaiser claimed to be a great admirer of his work and promised to send him an autographed photograph of himself, only added to his embarrassment.

"Your friends and I—we live in different worlds," he told Big afterward. "It's time I got back to the Sierra Madre and the Grand Canyon and the Big Horn where I belong. Europe may be good for some people, but it's sure poison for me."

A few days later he left for England to catch his ship for America. He reached London at the time that Buffalo Bill's Wild West Show was in town. In his London Wild West Show, Buffalo Bill had realized an old dream—to bring together riders from all parts of the world—South Africa, South America, Arabia, Russia, Mexico, and of course the United States. Instead of going to the National Gallery, as Big had urged him to do, Fred presented himself to Bill Cody, who already knew him by reputation. He drew South American gauchos in their tremendous cotton pantaloons, Russian Cossacks, and all the others, and he wrote to Big that the time had come when one no longer went to Wyoming to see cowboys and Indians. There were more in London.

After that he sailed thankfully for home.

A month later Big wrote him that the Russian government had reversed their decision. Official permission had been granted for them to cruise the Volga from Saint Petersburg to the Caspian. Fred wrote back that nothing would ever bring him to Europe again except a war. If war broke out, he would come running.

About the same time the Kaiser's photograph arrived, complete with brass frame, decorated with the imperial arms, and with what Fred claimed was sufficient "lingo" inscribed on it to give an Egyptologist work for the next two hundred years.

Fame had been multiplying in his absence, like moss on the stone that does not roll. The story of his and Bigelow's "expulsion" from Russia had preceded him, and, had spread around with pardonable exaggeration, giving him wide publicity. A new edition of Francis Parkman's classic, *The Oregon Trail*, with seventy-seven Frederic Remington illustrations, published by Little, Brown and Company, added to his mass audience.

There is a big difference between being known as a creative artist and an illustrator. Fred's reputation up to this time had been built almost exclusively on his magazine and book illustrations. It was a big event in his life therefore when, in January of 1893, the American Art Gallery held an exhibition of his drawings, water colors, and paintings. Ninety-six in all were auctioned off. Some sold for little more than the value of their frames, but his studies of Indians commanded fairly good prices. The highest sum paid was 410 dollars for a painting called "The Last Lull in the Fight," a variation of the "Custer's Last Stand" pictures, one of his favorite themes. This one showed three plainsmen fighting off Indians from behind the barricade of their dead horses. The total amount from the sale was over 7000 dollars, which not only covered the heavy expenses of the exhibition but enabled Fred to pay back certain debts, including 100 dollars he had borrowed from Big, and still realize a profit.

Like many another, Fred discussed that the more money he earned, the more it seemed he had to spend, and in spite of what was considered his phenomenal success, his budget did not always balance.

Even though he did not solve all his financial problems with his first exhibition, it was an important milestone for him, the beginning of his career as a painter of the Old West, instead of just an illustrator.

CHAPTER · *12*

Fred followed Missie out into the garden one morning, where she was gathering a few chrysanthemums for the house.

"I have decided something," he announced, plumping himself down on the grass. "I believe that a man should for one month of the year live on the roots of the grass, in order to understand for the eleven following months that so-called necessities are in reality luxuries."

"You weren't living on grass roots in Russia, my massive husband?" Missie asked him, smiling.

"On the contrary. I ate well," he said. "But all the time I was over there I felt as though I were a fish out of water—or vice versa."

"What would vice versa be?" she demanded, kneeling to examine a particularly lovely bloom.

"Like a bronco in the middle of the Atlantic, I guess." He grinned. "Missie, I have something to tell you."

"You're leaving," she informed him.

"How did you know?"

"I should be familiar with the symptoms by this time." She joined him on the grass, her arms full of flowers. It was one of the nice things about Missie that she was never so busy with household chores that she couldn't take time to listen to her husband's words of wisdom. "Where is it this time? Tell me about it."

"A place called 'Bavicora.' The end of the world," he said dreamily. "I've talked *Harper's* into letting me do some stories and pictures on a ranch in Mexico nobody in New York has ever heard about—two hundred and twenty-five miles northwest of Chihuahua . . . Do you want to hear more, Missie?"

"Yes, of course."

"This community was started in seventeen-seventy by the Jesuits. The good fathers carried on for seventy years, and then in eighteen-forty they were raided by the Apaches and all murdered. It was left to go to ruins after that, an outpost of civilization everybody forgot. About ten years ago it was redis-covered by an American cowboy named Jack Gilbert. He fell in love with it and decided he wanted it. The fact that the whole region was terrorized by Apaches didn't faze him. He's still there. 'Bavicora,' his hacienda, is one of the largest in all of Mexico . . ."

"How did you learn about it?" Missie asked.

"Oh, someone told me about it the last time I was in Mexico.

133

Since then I've been writing to Don Gilberto, as the owner is known thereabouts. I have an invitation to visit him."

"What do you expect to find there?" she asked finally.

He paused. "Why, people, I guess. My sort of people, that is."

He met the first of them when he got off the Pullman one chill early morning at Chihuahua—a little black man no more than four feet six, in enormous pantaloons and a big sombrero rolled up at the edges.

"Is you friend of Mista Jack's?" the apparition asked him.

"I am," Fred admitted.

"I take your check. Come this way."

This was the beginning of a fascinating friendship. The little man was called William and he had been a cook in a cow camp for the last thirty years, and claimed he could make a banquet out of the meat on a bull's tail. He also had a special genius for finding tobacco when everyone else was out.

The big Concord coach was overcrowded and had a habit of turning over at the slightest obstacle. On one occasion William had jumped off to get Fred's hat, which the wind had swooped off, and turned around to find the ground littered with boxes and debris and passengers. He regarded them all gravely. "If I'd been here I would be in two places for sure," he commented.

William had known romance, he told Fred. The girl had lived in the neighboring town of Brazos. She inspired him to save 400 dollars with which he intended to become a respectable citizen. He arranged to start an eating house for travelers in a little mud town and had even contracted for a stove and some furniture. But about that time his employer, who was holding his money for him, departed for parts unknown, 400 dollars and all. William entered into bankruptcy before his business got started, and lost his girl too. That was when he had attached himself to Don Gilberto, or Mr. Jack, as he called Fred's host.

Later Fred learned that William was the only man at "Bavi-cora" whose relations were equally easy and natural with everyone from the *patrón* to the smallest Indian baby. He even rated with the Chinese cook, who was suspicious alike of Texans, Mexicans, and Indians. He had courage too, for he had served out ammunition in Texas when his outfit was in a life-and-death tussle with the Comanches; on another occasion he held a crowd of starving Mexican teamsters off the grub wagon he had been delegated to guard.

The only feature of Western life that William had never been able to assimilate was the horse. Once in the remote past, he confided to Fred, he had trusted a bronco too far. It was the reason for his limping gait. Since then he had pinned all his faith on burros.

In spite of William's stories, the two hundred and twenty-five miles between "Bavicora" and Chihuahua turned out to be the longest miles on the map. They ran up long hills, dived into rocky canyons, stretched over burnt plains and across river beds thick with scorching sand. The Concord stage left them three-quarters of the way at Guerrero, and Fred, full of aches and pains, sprains and bruises, saw it depart with relief. The rest of the way, in the ranch coach, proceeded more smoothly, and at long last they came out of the tall mountain timber to look down at the great yellow plain of Bavicora. In another hour they were at the ranch—a great straggling square of mud walls enclosing two patios, with adobe corrals and outbuildings.

A bunch of cowpunchers, Americans and swarthy, mustached Mexican *vaqueros*, were gathered around the entrance as they drove up.

William ignored the need for introductions. "Right this way, Mr. Fred," he said, leading him into the guest room.

It was a surprise—a large room strewn with bear- and wolf-skin rugs, pictures and draperies on the walls, a good bed with

135

mattress and sheets, and in the corner an even more unexpected luxury—a washbasin and pitcher.

"Good Lord," Fred exclaimed. "I thought I was going to lead a primitive life."

"You be eating with Mr. Jack in his apartment tonight," William said. "Perhaps you ought to get sleep first."

"What's for dinner, William?" Fred teased. "Your banquet from the meat of a bull's tail?"

"Nassuh," said William without cracking a smile. "Charlie Jim, he does the cooking here at the ranch. I jest does it when we go campin'. You're going to eat right."

A few hours' rest did wonders for Fred's battered frame. It was still light when he awoke and he felt like a million. "Come in," he called in response to a knock.

A clean-cut, tanned, youngish man in store clothes that rested awkwardly on his muscular frame entered.

"Howdy, Mr. Remington," he said in a Texas drawl. "Welcome to 'Bavicora.'"

"Mr. Gilbert." Fred pulled himself up and offered his hand.

"You got me wrong, partner. Tom Bailey's the name. I'm the foreman. Jack sent me to get you."

As they walked through the patio, Bailey volunteered, "No one goes to the *patrón's* apartment with his hat on—no one except the *criada*, that is . . . The *criada* is the maid," he added as if doubtful of Fred's Spanish. "Here we are." He knocked at one of the adobe buildings just as the door opened.

Two men stood there, one old and bent and shabby, who was about to leave, the other tall and lean, browned to the color of the dark earth, with grizzled hair and clear, kind eyes. He wore tight riding trousers and an embroidered blouse with a colorful sash.

"*Muchas gracias, Patrón,*" the old man muttered.

"*Por nada.* It is nothing," the younger man said. "Until to-

136

morrow, Don Sabino." They shook hands and, as the old man turned to go, he touched his left arm with the old man's right in an affectionate manner. Suddenly Fred understood. The real power of Don Gilberto was not his skill, his bravery, or his daring; it was in his ability to make himself loved and needed. He was father as well as *patrón* of the hacienda.

"Come in, Mr. Remington," he called now in a hearty voice. "I'm mighty sorry to have kept you waitin'. Hope your trip up here warn't too gawdawful."

His speech was incongruous; the precise English of a Spanish grandee would have seemed more appropriate. Fred followed his host into his quarters, spacious and well furnished like the guest room, with a roaring fire in the huge fireplace. Next to it an old woman with a dark blue shawl around her shoulders squatted silently. The *criada*, Fred judged.

"How would a hot toddy go down?" Don Gilberto asked.

Fred allowed as how it should go down fine. His host spoke a few words in Spanish to the old woman who vanished, to return almost immediately with the steaming drinks.

"My house is your house while you are here," Don Gilberto said as they raised their glasses in a toast. "They have a saying for that in Spanish, and it comes from the heart. You know I never met an artist in the flesh before."

Fred was used to that sort of comment outside of New York and it always embarrassed him. To most Westerners an artist was a long-haired fellow who wore a flowing tie. He knew that his appearance was always a surprise.

"Guess you didn't expect so much flesh?" he asked.

"No, I didn't," his host admitted readily. "I expected some slicked-up city fellow. Now tell me what you'd like to see while you're here."

Fred knew that the owner of "Bavicora" still had not wholly accepted him, but that was not surprising. Don Gilberto had to

137

judge men as he judged horses. A stranger, even a well-recommended one, had to prove himself like anyone else.

"If you'll just let me make myself at home and get acquainted 'round here in my own way, that'll be fine," he said.

Don Gilberto smiled suddenly. "I have a feeling we're going to get along." He rose. "Now let's get some grub. I'm sorry we have no fancy New York food to offer you. Out here we eat steak, thick and rare."

"Nothing would suit me better," Fred murmured appreciatively.

In the days that followed, Fred did as he liked—and got himself acquainted with the ways of "Bavicora." Tom Bailey had been assigned to take charge of him, and did it with the same gusto that he performed his myriad of other duties, such as negotiating the sale of five thousand head of cattle, and "busting" a bronco no one else could touch.

By sign language and his rudiments of Spanish, he got better acquainted with the *criada*, who had some years before seen her husband killed by an Apache arrow at the front entrance of the patio. He visited the store, a room full of calicoes, buckskins, *riatas*, yellow leather shoes, guns, and all the other items that the populace of "Bavicora" considered the necessities of life. He chatted with Charlie Jim, Don Gilberto's Chinese cook.

He learned his way around the sprawling second patio, where the families of the Mexican *vaqueros* lived and where life went on as in any ancient Mexican village. In the doorways were the women in calico dresses and blue cotton *rebozos*, or shawls. Dogs and pigs wandered in and out and countless little brown children seemed to be ripening in the sun. Inside their homes, among the pottery and the stone *metates* still used for grinding corn, the men sat on mats on the floor, laughing and chatting and munching on tortillas.

138

As in the haciendas of old Mexico, a feudal state prevailed at "Bavicora." The *patrón* leased land to the Mexicans, who in turn were expected to follow him to war, which in this case had usually been against the Apaches. Though no door was ever closed, there were no windows. The Mexicans had long since learned that it was all too easy for the enemy to shoot through such openings, and accustomed themselves to doing without them.

No one bothered Fred, no one told him what he should or should not do. He drew out his sketch pad at will, sometimes sitting on a mudbank working at drawings of the adobe buildings against their background of broken hills.

One night the *patrón* gave a dance. One man had a harp, two had primitive fiddles, and another a guitar. The gaudily dressed *vaqueros* all came with their girls, and the way they dug up the dust from the dirt floor sent Fred into a paroxysm of coughing. Tom Bailey, who in addition to his regular duties, was master of ceremonies for occasions such as this, sang out over the fiddles, "Dance, you fellers, or you'll git the gout."

They all obliged except for Fred, who took refuge in a corner, happy with his sketch pad. Tom spied him out. "There's a woman who's prettier than a speckled pup," he said, indicating a young Mexican lass. "Why don't you put your twine on her?"

"Give me time," stalled Fred, and at the next opportunity he sneaked out the door, lest the invitation be repeated. For a long time he stood out on the plains, watching the dark silhouettes of the hills against the yellow sky, and listening to the distant howls of wolves competing with the music inside.

If the idea of dancing with a pretty Mexican girl terrified Fred, he was quite up to the ardors of a trip to the furthest outlying ranch on "Bavicora" to hunt and give the punchers time to "gentle" some steers for work-cattle. The party was composed of Don Gilberto, Tom Bailey, and another ranch foreman, an Indian hunter called Epitacio outlawed by his own tribe, several Mexican *vaqueros*, and of course Fred's first friend of "Bavicora," the indispensable William.

One day they scoured the plains for antelope. On another Fred received a lesson in "gentling" steers in the Mexican manner. This meant, he wrote later, that a steer would either be gentle or dead when it was over. To the layman the *vaqueros* seemed brave to the point of recklessness, but in reality they knew the nature of a bull thoroughly and could tell just when and where he was going to strike as precisely as a top-rate boxer can estimate the moves of his opponent.

In rainy weather they rode their mounts over wet rocks under the drip and drizzle of the mountain pines. They traversed vast ranges so remote that prospectors for silver or gold could hardly have worked a mine even had they escaped the vigilance of the Apaches and ventured so far. They rode past great crags and huge pillars of brilliantly colored porphyry rock cut into fantastic shapes by water and frost. The colors and the shadows impressed themselves in Fred's memory, so they could be recalled when he was once again in front of an easel.

It pleased him that the men he was with, hardened to this strenuous life, gave no indication that they thought he might weaken because of his bulk or his soft city living. It was a challenge, and Fred accepted it. All the same, there were moments when even the wild beauty around him and the rough male companionship that he loved most were not recompense for the aches of his body, the neuralgia that struck him at night, the painful shortening of breath, the all-enveloping fatigue. I'm getting old, he told himself. I'm only thirty-two, but my days are numbered.

He put away such melancholy reflections by kidding with William or extracting stories from his other companies—true or false, it didn't really matter—about days that were past.

140

The average day's ride began at six in the morning and lasted until four in the afternoon when the sun vanished behind the hills, or until they found water. Deer for venison they had in abundance, though even all William's culinary skill could not keep it from being a monotonous diet. But one after another their other supplies gave out—the flour, the sugar, the coffee.

One night they camped on a jutting crag, with water running in the canyon two hundred feet beneath them. For a hundred miles the mountains and plains lay out beneath them. It was a place more suitable for an eagle's eyrie than a camp. The night was frosty and the moon threw down a mellow light. In front of the campfire the Indian hunter related with gesture and swaying of body an account of a fight to the death with a rival band of Indians. When he had finished, one of the *vaqueros*, just as expressively, told the legend of the lost mine of Tiopa. The Jesuit fathers who discovered it, left a door of iron over the entrance before they fled from the Apaches, never to return.

A gigantic theater, thought Fred as he listened and watched, superb actors, a command performance such as all the fortune of kings and queens could not have summoned.

A few mornings later, when they were stopping on a giant grassy mesa, Don Gilberto drew up his horse next to Fred's.

"There they are over yonder," he said, pointing to the opposite crags.

"What?" asked Fred blankly, struggling to adjust his vision. Then he saw them, perched like dove cotes against the precipice. "Cliff dwellings!"

"Yep," said Don Gilberto proudly. "My discovery. They have been there for centuries. The paths are washed away, but our men climbed up with lariats the last time we were here."

"Are we going again?"

The *patrón* shook his head. The dwellings were only a quar-

141

ter of a mile distant, but it would take two days to reach them. Tobacco was running low, and for the men that meant the end of the trip. "There's nothing left there but dust and cobwebs anyway."

Still, it was with regret that Fred turned his pony from this view of an ancient civilization, an enigma that must wait still more decades for rediscovery.

He had had it, his month living on the roots of the grass which he had mentioned to Missie before he set off for Mexico. Not literally perhaps, but near enough to temporarily satisfy that urge that was forever forcing him to desert the comforts of New Rochelle and the pleasure of the table and the adulation of New York friends for a more primitive way of life.

CHAPTER · *13*

A windy day of March, 1894, found artist-illustrator Frederic Remington in a most unexpected place. He and Poultney Bigelow, in the company of a French captain, were riding Arabian steeds across the sands of the Sahara Desert headed in the general direction of Timbuktoo.

It had started back in the States a few weeks before. Fred had been working hard and felt, as was not unusual with him, that he needed a change.

"You don't look well," Big commented one day when he was visiting him at "Eudion." "You have a disease called Americanitis. A few days under the burning African sun will fix you up fine."

"Let's go," said Fred, forgetting all about his resolution never to cross the Atlantic again.

He had only the vaguest idea of African geography, and Big, who knew Europe so well, was not much better informed. They both knew that the Congo and the Nile were in Africa, and that France had some highly picturesque Arab troops somewhere along the northern edges of the continent, that there were fine horses to be seen there. But that was about the extent of it. Nevertheless within a few days, after packing a huge revolver and a monstrous pair of arctic galoshes, Fred was ready to embark on his second non-American adventure.

That a French-African official called *Le Capitaine du Moulin* had volunteered to act as their guide and host was an affair of chance. The captain and his French wife had shared their compartment on the train leading from the coast to the Atlas Mountains. Big had astonished the strangers by asking permission to light a cigar. Fred had increased their amazement by offering to move their luggage into a private compartment so that Madame would be more comfortable. The truth was that he made the suggestion because of his fear of women. The couple decided to stay, but Fred was spared the ordeal of making conversation with the chic young Frenchwoman because she spoke no English.

The captain and his wife were full of praise for the gallantry of the two Americans—so unlike Englishmen, they insisted, who wouldn't have thought of asking a lady's permission to smoke. As a result the captain invited them both to go with him to visit a great Arab chief. Madame, of course, would not accompany them on this strenuous journey.

That was how it happened that they were now on their way to meet one El Hadj Ahmed Ab d'el Kader ben el Hadj Moham-med—a long name and a long time getting there.

Fred was exultant. "This is a darn sight better than London, Paris, Berlin, and Saint Petersburg rolled into one," he exclaimed, his wide gesture taking in the gray blanket of sand and the ragged ridge of the Atlas Mountains in the distance. "Why, it's just like Arizona."

Poultney translated him to the captain, who seemed very pleased.

They had the desert pretty much to themselves, though once they encountered a camel train bearing dates and wool from the interior. It was escorted by Arab horsemen in white burnooses perched high upon tough and springy mustangs, balancing guns across their saddle bows. They eyed the strangers malevolently.

"I have an idea our lives are worth considerably less than a plug nickel to those guys," commented Fred as they passed on.

"Don't forget that France is supporting fifty thousand soldiers here for the express purpose of making this journey safe for us," Big shouted above the wind.

"A lot of good your statistics will do out here," Fred called back through mouthfuls of sand.

They had been journeying since sunrise. Sometime past noon the outline of a solitary horseman appeared on a rise of land in the distance. He rested motionless until they were close enough to see the whites of his eyes—an old man, perhaps seventy, who sat on his horse with the ease of youth. Over his long white burnoose he wore a black one of camel's hair.

"It is El Hadj Mohammed himself," exclaimed the captain.

He and the Arab chieftain exchanged greetings, then El Hadj rode over to the Americans, pressing the palm of his hand to theirs and touching his finger to his lips.

"He has accepted you as his guests," the captain told them.

The Arab asked where they were from and the captain told him, "From England."

"But we are Americans," protested Poultney.

"He knows of England," explained the captain. "He never heard of America."

144

It was indeed news to Fred that there was anyone anywhere who had not heard of America. He rode along in silence.

They pulled to a halt as though waiting for something. Then from out of an ambush sprang a cloud of Arabs, spurring their steeds into a breakneck gallop and charging wth such fury that it seemed inevitable they would ride over the small party. They swerved to the side to miss them by a hairsbreadth, their white burnooses swelling behind them in the wind like the wings of some great bird, their guns held high in the air. They turned and repeated the performance.

There was an exchange of a few words between the chieftain and the captain and the captain and Poultney.

"Fred," cried Big. "This show is for you. You're supposed to be an artist. Take your hands out of your pockets and sketch something. Our host is getting offended."

"You think I need to sketch a scene like this?" Fred demanded excitedly. "Boy, this is really something. Just tell the chief I won't forget a movement."

More words went back and forth and the chieftain nodded, still puzzled but willing to try to understand.

The squadron came toward them again, and then when quite close, brought their guns to their shoulders, aimed them toward Fred and his companions—and fired.

It was so realistic that Fred thought briefly this must be an insurrection and they would all be slain, but when the clouds of dust and smoke cleared away he saw there were no casualties. The Arab horsemen, resting motionless, were sitting proudly erect in their saddles.

They exchanged signs of friendship with the squadron then. Three of El Hadj's sons were in the band and the chieftain had them come forward. Two were grown men, athletic and soldierly. The third was barely nine and not big enough to shoot a gun from the saddle, though he rode his small horse as wildly and securely as the best of them.

They rode on to the encampment of the mighty El Hadj—about a dozen or so round tents of brown camel's-hair cloth. The entrances faced toward the inside of a semicircle, and along the front of them was a thick rope to which the horses were hobbled. The chief's tent was the largest. With a gesture he ushered them inside.

They were greeted by all the male members of his family, who stood solemnly in a row. Fred never did find out where his wives and his children were, though occasionally he heard the sound of women's laughter or the cry of an infant.

The tent was only some twenty feet across, but the rich Oriental rugs on the ground and the costly shawls about the sides and across the top showed it to be a royal mansion. The visitors and the family of the chief took places on the floor in a circle. Custom dictated that no servant should serve the food. Kitchen menials brought each dish to the tent door, where it was taken by a retainer who handed it to the chieftain. He served them all personally.

Plate after plate of highly spiced meat was passed around. To Fred each one varied only by the amount of sand that had seeped in, and he thought yearningly of the good "Bavicora" steak. When he thought the ordeal was over, the flaps of the tent door suddenly parted wide. El Hadj waved his hand, and his two eldest sons stalked in, bearing between them a kid, split from end to end on a pole the size of a canoe mast. It had been roasted whole in honor of the guests.

Following the example of the captain, Big and Fred seized their jackknives, peeled off pieces of meat, and ate it with their fingers. It proved to be succulent and delicious; Fred didn't have to pretend to enjoy it. Much to the gratification of the chieftain, he ate enormously, only rivaled in appetite by the host's nine-year-old son.

They were served coffee then in silver cups of exquisite workmanship. Afterward, with the chieftain's permission, they brought out their cigars. Religion forbade tobacco to the Arabs, who protected themselves from the forbidden fragrance by drawing their burnooses across mouth and nostrils.

Cushions were brought forth by the retainers and they all stretched out luxuriously. It was time for conversation. They overcame the language difficulty by the captain's translations of Arab to French, which Poultney reduced to English for Fred, and thus everyone was able to talk about all manner of things not connected with New York and publishers and art editors.

The visit to the Arab chieftain was the high point of Fred's African adventure, though there was a more publicized incident concerning the time Poultney and Fred wandered into a steam bath only to discover that they had landed in the women's quarters by mistake. They staggered out quickly, but the shrieks of the outraged women had already reached the streets. The two men were promptly surrounded by an angry mob of Arabs armed with sticks and knives, and were certainly in more danger than they had ever been in their lives. Poultney wrote both the Arab chieftain and the women's steambath episodes for separate articles, which Fred illustrated graphically after he returned to America.

The next year he went up to Canada on a hunting and canoeing trip with Julian Ralph and a couple of other New York aesthetes. Ralph gave one version of this trek in his book *On Canada's Frontier*. Fred described it in a story called "The Strange Days that Came to Jimmy Friday," Jimmy Friday being the half-breed guide who went along with these citified gentlemen. Fred illustrated both his own story and Ralph's book.

He went to Florida that year too, and was able to compare the cowboys there with the Western brand—another illustrated story. He went out to Yellowstone and made a tour with the soldier guards, exploring the far corners of the Park for signs of poachers. He met General Miles in Colorado and went bear-hunting with him in the Rockies. Such was the pattern of Fred's life. No one could ever solve the mystery of how he managed to travel so much and yet accomplish so much work too.

He arrived in Chicago in July of 1894, at the time the excitement of the Pullman Strike was at its peak.

With the years Fred had become more opinionated in his political utterances. In an unnecessarily virulent letter written to Big about this time, he expressed bitter hatred toward Jews, Chinese, Italians, "Huns," and "Injuns." He often voiced the opinion that the ills of the country came from the stream of foreign immigrants who were spoiling everything for the real Americans. His friends, even those like Augustus Thomas who disagreed with him most violently, tolerated such outbursts because of Fred's good humor, loyalty, generosity, and many other virtues. Missie, who never criticized him for his drinking or his long absences or his extravagances, staunchly opposed him in these matters.

"People are people," she told him firmly. "It doesn't matter what the color of their skin is, or what church they go to, or what country they come from. America is for everybody, not just for us."

"Sure, kid," Fred said. He never contradicted her.

But he didn't change. Like many of his military friends and some of the more snobbish members of the clubs he belonged to, he used words as symbols of his prejudices. The Pullman strikers, for instance, were a "mob," who opposed law and order. He never bothered to delve into their grievances, and wrote Big that their mass demonstrations were "hot stuff." He even did an article for *Harper's* called "The Affair of —th of July," depicting an imaginary pitched battle between the Chicago "insurgents" and the United States Army, with fighting and shooting at every street corner. Supposed to depict what would happen if the strikers got out of hand, it was one of his less successful attempts at fiction.

Another article about an imaginary situation in a lighter vein was "The Colonel of the First Cycle Infantry." Bicycling had become a fad in America in the 90's and both Fred and Missie had taken it up. Fred became an enthusiast when he learned that a strong bicycle didn't balk at his two hundred and forty pounds, as even the most hardy mounts were now likely to do. His bicycling inspired him to write about a "Cycle Infantry" that also managed to defeat a band of "insurgents."

Writing was still just a hobby to him, a background for his pictures. Apologetically he would explain to his friends that the only reason he did it was to teach people about the West. He would have been the first to agree that he didn't have the eloquence or the gift for turning a fine phrase that his friend Poultney Bigelow had. He was embarrassed when General Miles wrote him that he was a genius with a pen as well as with a brush and when old Mr. Harper compared his writing style to De Maupassant's. In spite of his reservations about his writing ability he was as pleased as punch when in 1895 Harper's issued his first book, *Pony Tracks*, consisting of a collection of his published articles.

He let nothing interfere with his tremendous output as an artist. His usual schedule was to rise at six, eat a hearty breakfast, usually including pigs' knuckles or lamb chops and innumerable cups of coffee, and then work straight through until three, when he might go for a ride or play tennis or indulge in some other form of physical relaxation. When there weren't guests, he might return later in the day to his easel. In spite of his mass production, everything he turned out had to be right by his standards, and for every finished piece of work there were usually dozens of discarded sketches.

"Why do you worry so much?" his friend and neighbor, Augustus Thomas, asked him once. "You know you're good."

"I know nothing of the sort," Fred retorted. "Moreover, Tommy, if I felt cocksure of anything about my business, I would begin to be afraid of myself."

He wanted to become expert in every medium, and alternated with pen and ink, charcoal, oils, and water colors. He even experimented with copperplate etchings, though this form interested him less than others. Many years later, collectors of "Remingtoniana" would consider his rare etchings as among their most valuable possessions.

In 1895, in spite of his tremendous popularity throughout America, Fred was still regarded with a certain disdain by fashionable New York art critics. They deplored the garishness of his colors. Furthermore, paintings that told stories, as his did, were not Art with a capital "A." The realistic details on which he prided himself was considered outmoded by those who returned from Europe as devotees of French impressionism. Such criticism made Fred indignant, and it also hurt him more than he would admit.

In this year he embarked on another medium that not only won over the critics but, perhaps more than anything else he did, gave him a permanent niche in American art.

Augustus Thomas dropped in on Fred one day as he was working out a sketch in charcoal to illustrate a short story by Owen Wister called "The Second Missouri Compromise." The caption for this particular drawing read " 'Don't Nobody Hurt Anybody,' said Specimen Jones," and it showed the inside of a saloon with one character in the foreground pointing his gun at some people. Fred had no models and was working completely from imagination and memory. Suddenly he rubbed out everything he had done.

"It's all wrong," he told Thomas. "Our hero is stealing the show."

He then made a new sketch from a different angle, as though in his mind's eye he had moved around the room he was portraying.

Thomas watched him wonderingly. "Fred, you're not a draftsman, you're a sculptor," he said unexpectedly. "You saw all around that fellow and could have put him anywhere you wanted him. They call that the sculptors' degree of vision."

"I'll tell you a secret," Fred confided. "I've always had a feeling for mud. It would be great to make something that time and moths couldn't touch."

Shortly after that, Thomas appeared one afternoon at the Remington home with a dark-haired man sporting a Vandyke beard whom he introduced as the Alsatian-born sculptor, Fred Ruckstull. He had just won a commission to do an equestrian statue, a gigantic affair that would have a place of honor in front of the capitol at Harrisburg, Pennsylvania. He was going to be working on it in New Rochelle that summer. Fred was interested immediately.

"A sculptor, eh?" he commented as he ushered his guests into his studio. "Tell me, Ruckstull, how do you go about making a statue? How did you get this commission? You're the man who can tell me just the things I want to know."

The sculptor explained that he had won his commission on the basis of a twenty-inch model. This summer he was going to make a larger model, about four feet high. After that he would be going to France to make the final clay model.

"You'll be able to see just how it's done," Thomas interrupted. "I've persuaded Ruckstull to set up a shack on the land back of my house, so we can all keep track of his progress."

"Great!" Fred boomed. "You're going to see a lot of me there."

True to his word, he showed up every afternoon around three to watch the sculptor at work. His eyes would follow every movement of Ruckstull's deft hands, and he asked questions about the steps necessary to create something that "time and moths couldn't touch." Usually he played the role of a disciple, but once in a while he had to protest the type of horse Ruckstull had selected—a monumental and picturesque Eastern breeder.

"You've got a handsome animal all right," he conceded. "But of course he wouldn't have a chance up against one of my wiry little Western ponies."

This sort of remark always led into an argument that went on for hours.

One day Ruckstull, returning from a trip to New York, stopped by Fred's place with a big package.

"For you," he said as he opened it up and spread out the contents on the table in Fred's studio—a modeling stand, clay, plastaline, wire, pliers, shears, and an assortment of wooden sculptor's tools. "This will get you started."

Fred's eyes bulged. "You're a prince, Ruckstull. Just the push I needed to get me started."

He spent all evening experimenting in making small figures out of the soft clay; after each unsuccessful attempt rolling and kneading the stuff back into its original shape and starting over, trying to get the feeling of working with solids and masses rather than flat surfaces.

Toward midnight Missie appeared in the doorway bearing a tray with coffee and sandwiches. "What are you doing up so late, Fred?" she scolded him lightly. "You need some rest . . ." She stopped short.

152

In a semicircle on the table in front of Fred stood a row of miniature horses, galloping, walking sedately with raised fore-legs, rearing, tossing their heads, and, leading the others, a bucking bronco with a tiny cowboy straining to keep his seat.

Fred looked up sheepishly. "I'm playing paper dolls." *

"Why, they're adorable!" Missie exclaimed. "I didn't know you could do that."

"I didn't either. You really like them?"

"I'm crazy about them." She leaned over his shoulder to study the little animals more closely.

"Not so bad for a first try, eh?" He reached over and picked up the little bronco. "I'll tell you a secret, Missie. This is the one I'm going to do first. I like the idea of immortalizing in bronze the ugliest creature God ever made."

The next morning Ruckstull showed Fred how to make an armature—the wire skeleton that would give support to his model—instructed him how to apply the moist plastaline over the armature in layers until he had built up the mass, illus-trated how to use the various tools, most important of which were his own fingers.

"You learn fast," he commented, noting that Fred was al-ready proceeding like a professional, removing bits of Plasta-line, smoothing out rough spots, digging out hollows, as though he couldn't wait to see his bronco emerge from its amorphous state.

Fred, intent on his work, did not answer. He was more than grateful for the older man's assistance, but once he had grasped the technique he wanted to go ahead in his own way. Already he had decided he didn't want to do the standard equestrian statues of the sort that so often adorn public parks and monuments. His would be small—not more than two or three hands high. And they would be cast in bronze; only that metal it seemed to him would give them real permanence.

When his plaster model of "The Bronco Buster," as he called his first piece, was completed to his satisfaction, Ruckstull sent him to Riccardo Bertelli of the Roman Bronze Works for the lasting. Bertelli protested volubly the difficulties of casting an animal that was standing practically upright on its hind legs.

Fred scoffed. "My next model is going to show a galloping horse with all four feet off the ground. What will you do then?"

The Italian craftsman glared at him. "I beg your pardon, Mr. Remington, I am not one of the Wright brothers."

There were some things that could be done in a painting or a sketch that just weren't feasible in sculpture.

Eventually "The Bronco Buster" was cast in bronze just as Fred had conceived it and was put on exhibition. It created a sensation. The art critic of *Harper's Monthly* wrote of Fred's first sculpture: "He has handled his clay in a masterly way, with great freedom and certainty of touch, and in a manner to call forth the surprise and admiration not only of his fellow craftsmen, but of sculptors as well . . . Mr. Remington has struck his gait . . ." Other reviewers and critics were equally enthusiastic.

The initial success spurred Fred to further efforts. One of these, "The Wicked Pony," which showed a bronco about to stamp on a fallen cowboy, aroused a great deal of speculation: no one could figure out how the cowboy was going to escape the pawing feet of the enraged beast. Someone asked Fred if the youth really had time to roll to safety. "He didn't," Fred said. "I saw it happen. The cowboy was killed."

Another favorite was "Coming Through the Rye," a more elaborate model portraying four cowboys dashing at full gallop and waving six-shooters over their heads. Here Fred had done what he threatened to Bertelli—one of the mounts really did have all four hoofs in the air, possible because it was supported by the rest of the composition.

Fred continued working with the Italian caster—supervising,

criticizing, arguing, demanding the impossible, and usually getting it.

One day Bertelli suggested they try the *cire-perdue* process. "What's that?" Fred demanded suspiciously.

Cire perdue was French for "lost wax," Bertelli explained. This was a method of casting known to the early Chinese and the Greeks, and brought to perfection by Benvenuto Cellini in the sixteenth century. It was widely used in Europe but was still virtually unknown in America.

"Never mind the history," Fred said. "How is it done and why should we use it?"

Patiently Bertelli recited the steps involved in the process. From the original model in plastaline, a plaster cast was made into which a more durable substance was poured to harden into another model. Once again a cast was made, this time of a gelatinous material. This second cast was then cut into as many small sections as the shape and form of the model required and a plaster cast made of each of these small pieces, which were fitted together like a jigsaw puzzle.

The next step was to paint the inside of this third plaster cast with a coating of melted wax, the wax to be of the thickness of the eventual bronze, after which the wax coating was oiled. At this point the outside plaster cast could be removed in its sections so that only the hollow wax replica of the original model remained.

The final stage consisted of placing a harder substance on the inside and outside of the wax model and baking it, so that the melted wax drained out by a system of tubes, and then pouring in its place the molten bronze. The bronze, its gold tone subdued almost to black by application of certain chemicals, would be the finished statue.

This method ensured the most accurate copy of the original model, Bertelli told Fred, and it also had another advantage. It was possible for the artist to make final corrections on the fragile shell of the wax model, painting upon it with a brush dipped in melted wax or smoothing away any projection that did not belong with a scapula or fingers.

"That I'll have to see for myself," Fred exclaimed.

They tried out the *cire-perdue* process on his model of "The Frightened Pony," which showed a pony rearing at a coiled rattlesnake. When the delicate, honey-colored wax model finally stood on Bertelli's workbench, Fred regarded it with something like awe.

"Go on," Bertelli urged him. "It's ready for the artist's final touch."

"The tail," Fred said. "It's not quite the way it should be." Tentatively he made a few new indentations with his thumbnail, and then slowly and with infinite care moved the still-warm wax to give the tail the proper swing. "I was scared silly it would break," he admitted afterward, breathing heavily.

"You have big hands," said Bertelli. "They look clumsy, but they have the skill of a surgeon."

Fred changed the position of the foreleg slightly then, and after that he decided to move the rattlesnake, lifting up the little string of wax and putting it back a fraction of an inch to the right.

"Great fun, isn't it?" he exclaimed, beaming proudly.

"You can make all the changes you like on each replica," Bertelli told him. "The only limitations are your time and your patience."

Time and patience—those were two things Fred had in abundance when it came to improving and perfecting his work.

In his sculpture he sought to follow the same principles that guided him in painting—realism down to the smallest detail, the evocation of movement in man and animal, the relating of a story. Oddly enough, the same critics who had sneered at his paintings for being too realistic outdid themselves in proclaiming that in his sculpture Frederic Remington had finally achieved artistic excellence.

Fred did some twenty-five pieces of sculpture in all during the next several years, and they were displayed in major museums throughout the country. None exceeded the popularity of his first, "The Bronco Buster." Two hundred and fifty bronze copies were cast before the model was destroyed and sold even then for a total of 62,500 dollars. This work became one of the most prized possessions of Teddy Roosevelt, for it was a gift to him from his Rough Riders after the Spanish-American War.

CHAPTER · *14*

In 1896 Fred was engaged by the tall, homely, young publisher of the New York *Journal*, William Randolph Hearst, to go to Cuba with Richard Harding Davis and report on conditions there. The dashing and handsome Dick Davis was three years younger than Fred and one of America's best-known newspapermen. Fred had corresponded with him five years before, while illustrating Dick's book, *West from a Car Window*. The trip that had inspired the book was Dick's one and only venture to the West. He admitted freely that he preferred taking a carriage down Fifth Avenue to riding a horse across the plains of Texas, and that he liked the food at Delmonico's better than the Western diet of beans and sourdough.

Despite their many differences the two men both had a flare for adventure.

"I have a plan for us, Fred," Dick said as the two of them were having a cold drink in Madame Beaulieu's Restaurant in

Key West, Florida, one sweltering afternoon. "I'm arranging to have a launch pick us up and take us to a rebel port in the Santa Clara province of Cuba. We'll sneak in without the knowledge of the Spaniards and get the real story."

"Bully," said Fred, using the favorite word of his sponsor, Teddy Roosevelt. "When do we start?"

"Tonight." Dick leaned over the table and spoke in a low tone. "Don't tell anyone you're leaving. I'll meet you at the foot of the pier at nine o'clock . . ."

That night with all the precaution of conspirators they boarded the light launch, but a sudden tropical storm came up when they were a few miles out to sea and the launch had to turn back. A few days later they tried it again, only to meet with a sea so rough that even the crew gave up hope and the Chinese cook set to work making a raft out of boxes and doors. They had to give up Dick's plan then and resort to the more prosaic method of booking passage to Havana on a steamer. This meant that when they arrived they presented their credentials to Spanish authorities and listened to the Spanish side of what was known in the States as "the Cuban problem."

What was "the Cuban problem" and why were Americans getting so excited about it?

Cuba was one of the last colonies Spain had retained from its once-vast empire. The year before, the Cubans had rebelled unsuccessfully under the leadership of the patriot, José Marti. Then another rebel leader, General Maximo Gomez had started a program of burning canefields, as disastrous to Cubans as to Spaniards. The Spanish crown retaliated by sending a new governor of Cuba, General Don Valeriano Weyler, who soon was nicknamed "Butcher" Weyler because of his "reconcentration" measures, which consisted in driving Cuban farmers into the cities and towns and destroying their farms, on the grounds that they might be aiding the rebels.

Fred had the chance of seeing first hand what was meant by reconcentration when, after a few days' stop-over in Havana, he joined Dick Davis in the small Cuban town of Jaruco. Dick's eyes were haggard.

"You won't believe what's happening here until you see it," he told Fred in a low, hoarse voice when he met him at the station.

They took a walk through the town. In the streets and on the plaza they had to wade ankle-deep in filth. There was dirt in the church too, which had been turned into a fort and was guarded by Spanish soldiers. Beggars, young and old, with hollow faces and outstretched clawlike hands, followed them. Others sat listless and stricken in front of ramshackle huts jammed one against another.

"How can any human being live like that?" Fred demanded in horror, as he fought off a feeling of physical nausea.

"You'll find that whole families of *pacificos*, and sometimes more exist, in each of those shacks," Dick told him.

Fred drew on his meager knowledge of Spanish. "*Pacifico*. That means man of peace?"

Dick nodded. "That's right. These beggars here were farmers who wanted only to cultivate their small plots and be left alone. Now they have nowhere to go, no way of earning a living. I'm told that in every town in Cuba it is the same story."

A little girl dressed in rags, her face and body showing the signs of starvation, darted up to them and held out her hand. Instinctively Fred reached in his pocket for a coin.

"Don't do it, Fred," Dick warned him. "I tried it too, but it's no use. We'd just be mobbed. Nothing we can give will make any difference."

They stopped to watch a funeral procession.

"Smallpox," Dick said shortly. "Yesterday I saw six coffins carried up the hill to the burying ground. Spanish soldiers as

159

well as Cubans. The Spanish military seem to have no more regard for their own men than for these other poor devils—or else they're just powerless."

"Tell me one thing," Fred said. "Why is Hearst so concerned about all this?"

Dick shrugged. "He's a good newspaperman. Right now he's meeting some stiff competition from Joseph Pulitzer and his *World*. The *Journal's* stories about Cuba, together with Hearst's editorials demanding American intervention from President McKinley, are fine for circulation."

"That's pretty cynical."

"It's realistic." Dick stuck a cigarette in his mouth and lit it as they turned their steps toward their hotel. "Of course Weyler claims that he couldn't do anything else—that Gomez is a bandit. But Hearst isn't interested in Weyler's excuses."

That night for the first time since he could remember Fred had no appetite for dinner.

He couldn't take the sights and sounds and smells of poverty and suffering too long. He sent his sketches onto Hearst from Havana, writing him that since his job was done and there was no war, he was coming home. Hearst promptly cabled him an amazing message:

REMINGTON. HAVANA. PLEASE REMAIN. YOU FURNISH THE PICTURES AND I'LL FURNISH THE WAR.

Another Hearst fantasy, thought Fred, and sailed for America.

There was more truth than poetry in Hearst's boast, though it took him a little time and a half-million-dollar investment to prove it. Though President McKinley was strongly opposed to involving the United States in a war at this time, Hearst continued relentlessly his efforts to arouse American indignation.

In February of 1897 Davis, who had stayed on in Cuba, sent him a story reporting that Spanish police officers had boarded the American steamship *Olivette* and searched three young

Cuban women suspected of carrying messages from the rebels! Hearst summoned Remington to illustrate this story. He wanted a drawing of a young Cuban woman undergoing the indignity of a search by sinister Spanish officers. Fred tackled the job reluctantly, for he didn't like to draw women and he didn't do it very well. However, it came near to creating an international incident.

The whole country was outraged. A Congressman resolved to launch a congressional investigation. Spain protested. At this point Joseph Pulitzer's *World* produced one of the three young women. She denied the *Journal's* interpretation of the story. It was true, she said, that the three of them had been searched, but it had been done quite properly by a police matron. No men had been present. The *World* next printed another scoop—an angry letter from Richard Harding Davis, pointing out that his article didn't say the women were searched by men. That was all in Hearst's and Remington's imagination. Davis never again wrote for the *Journal.*

For several days Fred was unhappy about his unwitting participation in this hoax, but he was much too busy to brood about it. In addition to his painting and his new love, sculpture, he had had another thin book published, *A Roger Ranger in the French and Indian War*, and was getting together material for a collection of his articles and stories to be entitled *Crooked Trails*. He was also at work on his most ambitious literary effort so far, a long short story called *Massai's Crooked Trail*, about an outlaw Indian, based on legends of Geronimo and half a dozen other Indian rebels.

In the midst of such projects Augustus Thomas phoned him around noon of February 16, 1898. "The Western Union agent just telephoned me that the United States battleship *Maine* has been blown up and sunk in Havana harbor," he said. "It means war."

161

"Ring off," Fred told him with unaccustomed rudeness. "I have things to do." A few moments later he was on the phone with Alden at *Harper's*, demanding, not asking, an assignment to cover the forthcoming Spanish-American War.

Later historians would come to the conclusion that the Spanish did not blow up the *Maine*. They had nothing to gain and everything to lose by starting trouble with the United States. But very few figured that out at the time. The seeds sown by Hearst and the *Journal* had sprouted. All America wanted war. Still, much to the disgust of Fred and others, President McKinley stalled, seeking to solve the "Cuban problem" with peaceful negotiations. It was more than two months following the *Maine* disaster, on April 24, that war with Spain became official— ironically enough after Spain had agreed to nearly all of the demands of the United States government.

Fred, who had fretted and fumed during this period of indecision, said good-by to Missie. "This is it, kid. This is what I've been waiting for all my life." When she didn't answer, he added anxiously, "You do understand, don't you?"

"Fred, I want to say something," Missie told him finally. "I've never objected to your trips West, because I know that the West has been your lifeblood and it has made you the great man you are. But Cuba's a different matter. You don't belong there."

He reassured her and left, taking off for Tampa with credentials from *Harper's* and the *Journal* as an artist-correspondent, and with an official letter from the Department of State, written at General Miles' request, to the effect that Frederic Remington should be extended every courtesy by the Diplomatic and Counselor Offices during his sojourn abroad. A curious document since where he was going he never came near any Diplomatic and Counselor Offices.

Fred found Tampa seething with reporters, artists, photographers, all as anxious as he to take part in the big event—the first time in history that a war had been so well covered by the press. Rufus Zogbaum, another Western artist whom Fred had known in New Rochelle, was there. So were Stephen Crane and Fred's childhood friend, Irving Bacheller (he had dropped the Addison), now a promising novelist, and scores of lesser lights.

But if the press was ready for war, the army was not. Men had to be recruited, trained, armed, equipped. General Miles, Commanding General of the Army, thought it would be folly to send raw troops to a tropical campaign in the rainy season and urged waiting until fall. At first President McKinley agreed with him.

Fred, like his fellow correspondents, passed his time between Tampa and Key West, hearing humors and discounting them. When he could stand inaction no longer he persuaded naval authorities to let him ship out on the battleship *Iowa*, captained by "Fighting Bob" Evans. For seven days the *Iowa* cruised ten miles off the Havana coast on the lookout for the main squadron of the Spanish fleet, in charge of Admiral Pascual Cevera. But no enemy ships were sighted and they returned to Florida.

The monotonous journey convinced Fred once again that he would never develop a deep love of the sea. To curb his restlessness he composed an article explaining his feelings. "I want to get dust in my throat, kick dewy grass, see a sentry pace in the moonlight, talk long of my tribe," he wrote out of his nostalgia and homesickness.

He was back in Tampa when, on May 29, word came through that the United States Flying Squadron, which included the *Iowa*, had finally located Cervera's elusive squadron in the port of Santiago, and had it securely blockaded there. Fred had little time to regret that once again he had barely missed a crucial event, for preparations were being rushed now for the army's transportation to Cuba.

Fred found out that two cavalry squadrons were obliged to

leave their mounts behind. He went to General Miles indignantly: "General, I wonder who is responsible for this order to dismount the cavalry?"

General Miles raised his eyebrows. "What's the matter? Don't the men want to go?"

"They'd go if they had to walk on their hands," Fred admitted. This was the end of his first and only attempt to interfere in army matters.

On June 22 the Fifth Army Corps, in the charge of corpulent and capable Brigadier General William R. Shafter, arrived in sight of the Bay of Daiquiri, eighteen miles down the coast from Santiago. Fred, aboard the *Seguarança* along with the general and a host of other correspondents, stared out at the open space beyond the beach and felt this was the greatest moment of his life. The landing, as Richard Harding Davis described it later, was a gala affair, resembling more a boat race than a wartime invasion. The most surprising thing about it was that, though they were in full view of a Spanish blockhouse, not a shot was fired at them, the reason being, as was discovered later, that the Spaniards had fled.

General Shafter's plan was to move his men on to Santiago. There was only one route—a wagon road that led through the jungle down to the port of Siboney eight miles away, and then across the San Juan hills the rest of the way. The first afternoon General Lawton with his men was sent on ahead. Fred, sitting on a hill, watched them go, each soldier shouldering his rifle with apparent unconcern of impending peril.

For himself he intended to stick with the Sixth Cavalry, but when the next morning he found they had not received their marching orders he decided to go on by himself. He had with him his canteen, a rubber poncho, sketch pads, his six-shooter, and some hard biscuit. The jungle through which the winding road led him was green and beautiful. It was also intolerably hot. Walking was not Fred's favorite sport. Though he was not yet as stout as the three-hundred-pound General Shafter, it was hard going for him. A group of cavalry orderlies caught up with him, and their company inspired him to keep up the appearance of enjoying the hike. Frequently they passed Cuban rebels, their ponies loaded with the heavy clothing abandoned by American soldiers who had proceeded them. There was no sign of Spaniards. When they reached Siboney, it was raining in torrential sheets. Fred and a fellow correspondent, the writer John Fox, stretched one of their ponchos out on the soft mud, covered themselves with the other—and tried vainly to sleep.

"Say, Frederic, are you subject to malaria?" Fox asked out of the darkness.

"Probably," said Fred. He had felt a cold coming on all day. "My bones tell me I'll end up with congestion of the lungs. Can you suggest a remedy?"

"Surely," Fox said drily. "The fare to New York."

The next morning they woke to find that Siboney was being set up as a field hospital. The invisible enemy had materialized at Las Guasimas, a few miles inland, and the Americans had received their first burst of gunfire. The walking wounded, and others on stretchers, were already arriving. Thus Fred had his first glimpse of warfare—not in the glory of battle but in its terrible casualties.

An invalided officer made him a present of a horse he was no longer able to use, a well-mannered animal from Colorado. Fred fell in love with her at sight, as he had with Terra Cotta so many years before. He rode off to find the front, glad that he no longer had to depend on his two feet for transportation.

Two miles north of the road to Santiago he approached El Caney Hill, where Capron's battery was laying guns to begin shelling the enemy's stone fort, and—from a distance—watched the battery knock holes in the Spanish stronghold, while the infantry from the jungle exchanged fire with the enemy in their trenches below the fort. He rode down a road jammed with troops back to El Paso Hill, in time to witness Captain Grimes' battery being dragged in place to start its assault.

Then, suddenly, he was in the thick of things, with bullets whizzing near. Though he saw men collapse and fall all around him, he still couldn't believe he was in personal danger.

Someone yelled at him, "Get down, old man, or you'll catch one."

He obeyed reluctantly, giving his mare a comforting pat.

"Modern rifle fire is rough on horses," a cavalry officer near him commented. "They can't flop themselves on the ground like starfish as we can." He persuaded Fred to tie his horse with theirs in a small sheltered hollow.

He followed the ever-lengthening march and from behind a small bank under a big tree watched men coming out of the protection of the jungle, dashing across the wide field toward a hill, stumbling and falling under a grueling fire. Though he didn't know it, this was the beginning of the famous attack on San Juan Hill.

He left his outlook post and went down to a creek, following it out into the scrub. Bullets cut and clicked around him as he dashed across an open space, and he heard the "wheet" of a Mauser next to his ear. He dropped into the tall guinea grass, crawling to the shelter of a mango tree. Somewhere he lost his sketchbook but he didn't go back for it. He found he was sharing a small hollow with an officer.

"Is this thing allowed, Colonel?" he asked with mock gravity as the shrapnel whizzed over their heads.

"I wouldn't advise you to go out there and try to stop it," the colonel said.

He couldn't stop it, but his job was still to see what was going on. He found another lookout where he had a clear view of the fort on San Juan Hill. As he watched, a handful of blue-clad soldiers mounted to the top and planted an American flag there. At that moment the shellfire seemed to stop—or at least it was drowned out by the rousing cheers. It was the one thrilling moment in a ghastly nightmare.

In newspaper accounts of the fighting in Cuba, Theodore Roosevelt's First Volunteer Cavalry, better known as Teddy's Rough Riders, stole the show. The Rough Riders were the only soldiers who wore summer khaki instead of the uncomfortable blue woolen uniform of the Regulars, the only outfit competently equipped and armed. They were made up of mounted riflemen, Western plains riders, college men, former New York mounted police, and even Long Island polo players, and an aura of glamour enveloped them, causing some resentment among the Regulars. Charles Dana Gibson summed up the situation in a cartoon showing a soldier bitterly explaining to a girl: "No, I ain't no hero. I'm a Regular."

Fred saw both Regulars and Rough Riders in action; they were all soldiers to him, and brave. Later one of the Rough Riders, Theodore Miller, wrote in his journal that he owed his life to Remington and another correspondent; they had carried him back to the field hospital after he was wounded.

But when Fred described the attack on San Juan Hill in his *Harper's* article, "With the Fifth Corps," he wrote: "San Juan was taken by infantry and dismounted cavalry of the United States regular army." Nowhere in this article, a factual account of what he witnessed, did he mention the Rough Riders or Theodore Roosevelt in connection with San Juan Hill. Which makes it all the more strange that the best-known picture he ever did was "The Rough Riders at San Juan Hill."

Every American schoolboy knows this painting, which shows a detachment of Rough Riders led by Colonel Roosevelt advancing up the hill, silhouetted against dark green shrubs and trees. It was one of the few times Fred portrayed a celebrated person. Colored reprints were widely circulated. It was used as an illustration for Theodore Roosevelt's article about the Spanish-American War in *Scribner's* magazine. Later it was said that this painting was responsible for Roosevelt's being elected President. Years afterward Fred told friends that he hadn't seen Roosevelt at San Juan Hill, that he had in fact been hired to do the painting after the war to further Roosevelt's campaign for the position of New York State governor.

Much would be written about the Cuban campaign later, about officers vying with each other for power and prestige, about inefficiency and mismanagement and callous disregard of human life. This was not Fred's concern. What he wanted to do and what he succeeded in doing, by his article and by the illustrations made at the time, was to show what the war was like from the point of view of the men who participated in it.

After San Juan was taken, Fred headed back to headquarters through a jungle filled with wounded men. He found his Colorado mare unharmed where he had left her, the only horse that was not killed. But he was unable to mount her. Fever, which took even more casualties than the bullets did, had struck him. For an entire day he lay on the ground in the intense heat, staggering to his feet only to drink deeply, and very unwisely, of the dirty water in a nearby creek.

In a daze he watched reinforcements going toward the front, realizing with dismay that his part in the campaign was over. All he could do was to join the sick and wounded, the "broken spirits and broken bodies," who were dragging wearily to the rear.

Sick as he was, he still found strength to exchange notes with several of his fellow correspondents also waiting for passage back to America. One of them, a novelist, announced he was returning to complete an opus on "The Romance of a Quart

Bottle." Another said that in the future he would devote his energies to a treatise on the flora and fauna at Bar Harbor, Maine. As for Fred, he murmured feverishly that henceforth he would concentrate on painting dining-room furniture.

He had had his war but it hadn't been up to his expectations. He had seen heroism but he had also seen suffering and misery and death. It didn't take him long to regain his health once he was back in Missie's care, but he would never again write to Big about how he hoped for a real war so he could join it. He had, in this respect, grown up.

CHAPTER · *15*

Early in 1907 a young journalist named Perriton Maxwell took a train up to New Rochelle to interview the almost legendary Frederic Remington for a series on great American artists which he was doing for *Pearson's* magazine. In his pocket was a copy of a letter written by President Theodore Roosevelt that would lead off his article.

On the way he debated whether or not to show this letter to the artist. It was high praise indeed, saying that all Americans owed Remingon a debt of gratitude, and that the soldier, the cowboy and rancher, the Indian, the horses and the cattle of the plains would live in his pictures and bronzes for all time. In the end Maxwell decided he wouldn't bother showing Remington the letter. Such compliments would be old stuff to him, and he might misconstrue the journalist's action as an attempt to curry favor.

A cab driver drove him up the entrance and deposited him

at the door of the big, sprawling mansion. The woman who answered his ring was small and slender and her delicately chiseled face was still young, though her hair was snow white.

"Oh yes, Mr. Maxwell. My husband is expecting you. Won't you come into his studio? He'll be down in a few minutes." Her voice was pleasant and gracious.

Maxwell had heard of the Remington studio, with its double doors so wide and high that a fully mounted cowboy could ride in. It was as fabulous a place as rumor had indicated, the walls lined with all the Indian and cowboy souvenirs making up a collection that was probably the best in the country to be found outside of a museum. He had time to examine it while waiting, and he was struck by the fact that there were a few items of non-American origin: an Algerian rifle inlaid with ivory, an African spear, and several swords and daggers obviously of Russian workmanship, a burial urn, with a label attributing it to the fourteenth-century Aztecs, and a pewter communion pitcher from Nova Scotia.

"Howdy there, Maxwell."

He turned to greet his host and saw a man of elephantine bulk, not really fat but huge and superbly muscled, broad-shouldered, and big-fisted. His hair, slightly thinning on top, and his mustache were light brown, his complexion florid, and his face unlined in spite of his forty-six years. He wore a conventional business suit.

They shook hands.

"Sit down and tell me about yourself," the artist said. "Have a cigar."

As soon as they were comfortably settled, Maxwell evaded the first order by asking his host what he thought of Indians and cowboys today.

Remington was launched at once. "Cowboys!" he boomed out. "There are no cowboys any more, just the tame hired man who

170

herds cattle for his monthly wages and lives for weeks at a time in store clothes. The real cowboy disappeared with the advent of the wire fence. As for the Indian, he became extinct thirty years ago. I mean there are so few of him he doesn't count."

"You would say then, Mr. Remington, that the West of the roistering cowboy and the hate-inflamed Indian are no more than a ghost conjured up from the past?" Maxwell pursued the subject.

The big artist nodded. "I now paint things which I saw as a youth or which I heard about from men who took an active part in the stir of the early West. You see when I started this business, I had not only lack of information to combat, but the misinformation of the dime novels to live down."

Maxwell tentatively brought up the subject of other Western artists. Charlie Russell, the "cowboy artist," had once told somebody of being snubbed by Remington when he was in New York. There had also been a controversy between Charles Schreyvogel and Remington over Schreyvogel's painting, "Custer's Demand," which Remington had called "half-baked stuff," claiming that the Indian and soldier clothing was incorrect. But Mrs. Custer herself had defended Schreyvogel and it turned out that Remington was only right in part. On the other hand, he had a reputation for being very generous with advice and praise to young artist friends. Maxwell was curious to know what he would say about his rivals, but Remington was noncommittal:

"The younger men who attempt to portray the West must get their material from older artists, since the typical figures of the plains are as remote as the Civil War or the Paleozoic period. It makes it difficult for them." He added that of course many of them had sound drawing technique and good sense of color.

"Have you ever regretted that you didn't go to the Continent to study, Mr. Remington?"

"I'll tell you a secret, my boy. I'm rather an egoist by nature.

That is, I'd rather be myself with all my shortcomings than live in the shadow of some great European master I had unconsciously sought to imitate."

Maxwell's questioning brought out further incidents of the artist's career: his first published drawing in the *Yale Courant*, "a wretched little smudge"; the first one for *Harper's*, "a very bad drawing . . . I should rather not have it dragged from its well-deserved obscurity."

Fred paused. "The real thrill was when *Outing*, which was run by Poultney Bigelow, paid me ten dollars apiece for some pen-and-ink sketches. Ten dollars meant a lot to me in those days."

"There's quite a jump between that and the—is it twenty-five-thousand-dollar—annual retainer which *Collier's* pays you now for your double-spread color prints?" Maxwell ventured.

Remington ignored the implied question about his present financial arrangements with *Collier's* and took off on another angle. "When *Collier's* put me under contract for exclusive rights to everything I produced, they agreed to pay me six thousand a year. It was less than I had been earning free-lance, though of course I could sell the paintings after they had reproduced them. But the big thing for me was that for the first time a magazine was paying me in advance to choose my own subjects. That pleased me no end."

Maxwell had been going over back issues of *Collier's* in preparation for the interview, and he reeled off some of the paintings that had first been reproduced there: "The Pioneers," "The Gathering of Trappers," "Emigrants," "Night Attack on Government Wagon Train," "The Bell Mare," "Evening on a Canadian Lake." The issue in which the latter had appeared, on March 18, 1905, had been labeled the Remington Number and had been completely devoted to different phases of the artist's work.

"It must be quite exciting to realize that, all over America, families are waiting for their weekly magazine to see what the next Remington is."

The artist shrugged this off. "I get a lot of letters," he admitted. "The trouble is, I feel obliged to answer them all. I'm not as young as I used to be."

Maxwell asked him, rather impertinently he feared, if he was happier now than when he was getting ten dollars a sketch from *Outing*.

Remington did not take offense. "I enjoyed some of my art jobs in those days all right," he said. "Among other things, I illustrated Theodore Roosevelt's cowboy articles at a time when most people didn't know whether cowboys milked dairy cattle or fought in the Revolution." He smiled wryly. "I guess I knew more about cows than I did about drawing."

"But your real love is the army, is it not?" Maxwell asked then.

Remington didn't say anything for a moment. When he was not talking, there was a curious repose about this big man, as though he were some great animal looking out on the world through sleepy eyes.

"Frankly, I know very little about the army as it is right now," he said finally. "I have had nothing to do with soldiers since the war in Cuba. I only knew the soldier as part of my West, and the West and the soldier closed together."

They talked about his writing. "I'm through with that," he told Maxwell. "I suffered agonies doing *John Ermine of the Yellowstone*. That was a novel about a young white man who was raised as an Indian. The happiest moment of my life was when I finally wrote down those two sweet words, 'The End.' "

"I saw the play at the Manhattan Theatre. Louis Shipman did the dramatization?"

Remington grimaced. "The less said of that the better. It was

173

rather a flop. The critics were against it because of the unhappy ending. You know, I think it's the only time I ever put a heroine in a story."

"You've had eight books published, haven't you? Many a writer would consider that a lifetime work."

"I repeat, I do not consider myself a writer. If I could do something like *Trilby*, that would be different. I wrote my only fan letter to Du Maurier about that. He never answered me though. I also think that Shaw's *Man and Superman* is a great show."

Curious choices for a man dedicated to Western lore, thought Maxwell. He went on with the interview. "Of course books of your writings aren't the only ones you've had published. There are the *Collier's* portfolios, your *Frontier Sketches, Bunch of Buckskins*, and *Done in the Open* with the verses by Owen Wister to go with your paintings and the introductions about you."

"He uses real flowery danguage, don't he?" said Remington, purposely ungrammatical. "From now on I'm going to devote myself to painting and sculpture. There's not time enough left to paint and model all I would like to—even if I lived to be a hundred. Which I should say is doubtful."

The interview was over then and Maxwell rose to go. But before he left, he asked the artist for a photograph of his summer place on Chippewa Bay.

The sleepy look left his host's eyes. " 'Ingleneuk'?" he exclaimed. "There are only five acres of it, but it is the finest place on earth. Bless your soul, it couldn't be photographed at any angle. It is solidly screened from view on all sides by the densest growth of trees along the Saint Lawrence."

When Fred and Missie had first moved to New Rochelle, it had seemed in the country. But gradually other New Yorkers had pressed in on them, and Fred got the feeling that civilization was fast encroaching here on his private domain as it had on his West. One day he had looked out the window to see his next-door neighbor at work tearing down a picturesque old wall that marked the border of their estates.

He stormed out. "What do you think you're doing?"

The neighbor explained that he was tearing down the ugly relic as part of his scheme to modernize his own place.

Fred glared at him. "Well, sir, if I had my way I would send you to jail."

A few moments later his anger had passed and he was chatting pleasantly with the neighbor. But the thought remained that he wanted a real retreat, a place no one could spoil for him. As a result he had bought a small island in the St. Lawrence, which he had christened "Ingleneuk."

From then on he was there every year from March to October except for his briefer and briefer Western trips and for occasional sorties up to the Pontiac Club in Canada to do some hunting. He looked forward to his stay at "Ingleneuk" like a schoolboy. Missie liked it too. They had a large house with eight bedrooms—for while Fred wanted to be away from civilization, that didn't necessarily mean he wanted to be away from people, and friends were always welcome. There was also a front parlor and a back parlor and a dining room with wood-paneled walls. The kitchen was apart from the main house. There were no horses, for riding was a thing of the past for Fred.

His favorite pastime now was canoeing; he had several, trim and sturdy, made by Henry Rushton of Canton. When he got his huge frame into one of them it sank almost to water level, but there was no danger of capsizing. He also liked to go bass fishing with Charlie Denner, a rugged Down-Eastern lake captain, who had the next island, and sometimes he would go jack fishing at night with the local fishermen, armed with torch and spears. He did a painting of these night fishermen which hung in

175

the "Ingleneuk" dining room. When island life palled on him, he took off to shoot partridge on the mainland.

Missie talked him into getting a motor launch and sometimes she and her sister Emma got a local youth to run them around the different islands, paying calls on their neighbors. But Fred viewed the launch with suspicion. One day he took it out and when it stalled in the middle of the bay, a fisherman rescued him.

"I'll give you the dang thing for a cup of tea," Fred told him. He stuck by his bargain too.

Another story the islanders told about him had to do with the time that Congressman Merritt, who was about Fred's size, came for a visit. They laid a wager as to which one could eat and drink the most. The contest took place out on the end of the dock, and they ate and ate and finally the dock began to sink until they were up to their waists in water. It was never decided who won the bet.

The small boys on the bay, among them Captain Denner's son Henry, knew Fred as a friendly, hearty sort of man, who always dressed in loose khaki clothes and was never too busy to stop and show them his Indian costumes and the other fascinating things he had brought back from the West. Naturally they knew he painted. He was always doing it, sitting out in his open studio in front of his easel with his palette of colors. But the children had no idea, as they sat around on the grass, wriggling their bare toes and eating the sandwiches Missie provided, of the extent of his fame.

By this time Fred counted among his always-increasing intimates the top men in politics as well as those in the army. He still corresponded regularly with Teddy Roosevelt, who was forever urging him and Missie to come down and have dinner at the White House, and lamenting that Fred wouldn't "do" the Navy with the same gusto with which he had done the cavalry. With that wish in mind, he had once taken Fred on a three-day

176

cruise on his *Model Squadron,* but Fred had staunchly refused to be seduced by the wiles of Neptune.

Buffalo Bill wrote to him too, and once asked as a special favor if Fred could see his way clear to illustrate a book of poems written by one of his relatives. Fred was on good terms with Secretary of War Daniel Lamont. In an odd reversal of their positions, General Nelson Miles wrote for a favor. Would Fred use his influence with the Secretary to get him to counteract certain new legislation prohibiting private soldiers over thirty-five from re-enlisting in the Army—a ruling that the general considered cruel and unjust.

His annual trips to the West had become a chore for him in spite of the increased comfort of traveling. In his letters to Missie he confided what he did not say to others—how unbearable he found the heat and the dust, the dreariness of the small Western hostelries, the nuisance of washing out his own clothes in a hotel-room washbowl, his boredom at the social functions that courtesy required him to attend. The life of an artist in search of the beautiful is not easy, he wrote her on one occasion with heavy irony.

"Eudion" was becoming less and less the place he called home, and early in 1909, after nineteen years' residence, he sold it, to buy a fifty-acre farm on the outskirts of Ridgefield, Connecticut. It was an exciting venture, but it proved a costly one too. Before the new house was built, he had to put his beloved "Ingleneuk" up for sale—which he had once said he would not dispose of for 475,000,000 dollars. To his relief the buyer was John Howard, a boyhood chum from Ogdensburg, who had made money in the coal business. Fred had never sacrificed old friends for new ones; they had remained close all these years. He had the comfort of knowing that "Ingleneuk" would still be a haven for him. But he was not to be able to enjoy Howard's hospitality.

177

In spite of the nightmare of moving and installing themselves in their new home in the midst of painters, carpenters, and paper hangers, Fred found time to do some lovely paintings that year. He had finally discarded the bright oranges and reds that his critics had deplored in his earlier works, and turned to softer hues. That was the year he did "Apaches Listening," portraying a group of mounted Indians motionless on a gray mesa, with pale yellow sands and snowy peaks in the distance. He also did his celebrated "Sun Dance," showing the cruel training that went into the making of Indian braves, a picture that he had wanted to do for a long time but which he was convinced would never sell because it would give people "the horrors." He turned from Western scenery that year too, long enough to do "Hauling in the Gill Net," a scene of two fishermen in a canoe, located near Chippewa Bay in the Saint Lawrence.

Strangely enough, in these months he also experimented in pastels, somewhat along the lines of the French impressionistic school, which he once scorned. His "Sentinel" showed a bearded frontiersman, with high boots and shirt reflecting the pale green of the thick turf, against a covered wagon of violent hue. The last painting he ever did, "Around the Campfire," also in quiet tones, showed four cowboys squatting in front of their bunkhouse, possibly swapping yarns of great Indian battles of the past. A rifle, like a symbol of the danger they no longer faced, lay propped against the bunkhouse wall.

In and around Ridgefield, Fred swiftly became one of the most prominent citizens, and easily the largest, for he now weighed about three hundred and fifty pounds. The Remingtons entertained extensively, and every afternoon he would be seen out driving in his two-wheeled trap or in his one-horse carriage, pulled by a little brown and white pony, or in a larger wood-paneled seater, which the other horses from his stable pulled.

In November of 1909 he got a note from General Miles in

Washington which began, "My dear old friend," and which complained that he had not seen Fred for an age and wanted to see him very much. Poor fellow, he must be getting old, Fred reflected. The general, military and formal in his personal relations as in his profession, had never before written in this vein.

On the 20th of December he went to New York to arrange for an exhibition of his pictures in the Fifth Avenue Gallery. He wasn't feeling up to par, and as he left the gallery he was seized with acute pain in his left side. He managed to hail a cab and told the driver to take him to the station. On the way the pains grew worse and he instructed the driver to drop him at a hotel instead. Evidently something he had eaten hadn't agreed with him, he told himself. In any case he didn't feel like a train journey.

He felt better the next morning, but the pains started again on the ride up to Ridgefield. As soon as he got home he went right to bed. The next day Missie, over his protests, insisted on calling Dr. Lowe, their local physician.

"What's the matter with me, Doc?" Fred asked, forcing a grin.

"Before I answer that question I'd like to have a couple of my colleagues look you over," the doctor told him.

Two more physicians were summoned—one from Danbury and another from New York City.

Fred groaned as the three of them gathered around his bedside. "What have I done to deserve all this attention?"

"You're a big man. You need lots of doctors," Lowe said.

"All right. What is it?"

"You have appendicitis, my boy," he was told. "We're going to have to operate."

"Go right ahead," Fred said, cheerfully enough. "The sooner it's over with, the better. I thought it might be something serious."

But a routine operation such as the one for appendicitis can be serious with a patient the size of Fred.

The operation was performed in his home on December 23. After it was over, Dr. Lowe took Missie aside. His face was grave. "The pain will be relieved temporarily," he said, "but I must tell you the truth. Peritonitis has already set in. We can only hope."

On Christmas morning Fred felt fine. He even threatened to come downstairs to see the presents opened. Missie and her sister Emma, who had come to spend the holidays with them, compromised by bringing his presents up to his bedroom.

He made jokes and was very gay.

"Missie," he said suddenly, "did I ever tell you what you remind me of? You remind me of a Dresden doll. You didn't know that, did you?"

She leaned over and put her hand on his forehead. "You must really be sick to be paying me compliments."

"Why, you're crying," he said. "What are you crying about?"

Shortly after that he was in a coma.

When the doctor told them there was nothing more to be done, Missie sent a telegram to a friend in Canton to let his relatives, the Sackriders, know that her husband was sinking fast. Then she resumed her place at his bedside.

On the morning of December 26 it was snowing, a snow as thick and heavy as any Fred had known in his Western winters. It was during that snowstorm that his spirit went to join the prospectors, cowboys, trappers, Indians, Texas Rangers and Canadian Mounted Police, the United States Cavalrymen, and all the other characters of the Old West to whom his paintbrush had given immortality.

CHAPTER 16

EPILOGUE

In the years following his death, Frederic Remington's prestige continued to grow. John Howard and George Hall, another prominent Ogdensburg citizen, put up money to buy the famous old Parish house, where Ameriga Vespucci, a direct descendant of Amerigo Vespucci, according to legends about her, had lived in seclusion for many years. This was set up as the Remington Art Memorial, to house the Remington Indian Collection and the best of his paintings and sculpture. Missie and her sister Emma moved to Ogdensburg to take charge of it.

Elsewhere, museums and private collectors from Texas to Montana and from New York City to San Francisco vied with each other for prints, paintings, sketches, and even his personal letters. Though Fred had destroyed many of his canvases—he was never satisfied with his past efforts—there was still enough for all. When he died at the age of forty-eight, he had completed over twenty-seven hundred drawings and paintings which had appeared in over forty periodicals and in one hundred and forty-two books—eight written by himself.

In Ogdensburg, Missie sometimes gave lectures on the Indian collection, surprising everyone with her knowledge and her appreciation of it. The collection was housed at the Memorial until 1957, when it was sent to the Buffalo Bill Museum in Cody, Wyoming.

For the people of Canton, Remington continues to be a living memory, and they are still disappointed that the Memorial was set up in Ogdensburg rather than in the town where he was born. With the possible exception of novelist Irving Bacheller, he was their most important citizen. His exceeding generosity to his old friends was revealed after his death, for a good percentage of the population have somehow or other inherited a drawing or a sketch, a rough of one of his popular *buckskins*, or a painting on a piece of red velvet of a German Uhlan. Sometimes when an art dealer comes to town, they bring out these treasures and demand to know how much they are worth in dollars and cents. But they rarely sell. "If it is worth nothing there is no use selling; if it is valuable I want to keep it," one woman commented, a sentiment which is embraced by many.

In 1939 the United States Post Office authorities approved the inclusion of Frederic Remington in the Artist Group of their Famous American Series, using the same photograph that appeared in *Pearson's* magazine of October, 1907, on a ten-cent stamp. September 30, 1940, was selected for the first day of sale, and Canton was granted the honor of conducting the sale because it was his birthplace. The Canton Post Office was swamped with mail for several weeks prior to the sale and was forced to engage twenty additional employes. In all, 116,219 covers received the official "First Day of Issue" cancellation, which was good for a small town, and an indication of their enthusiasm over the event.

The controversy over whether Frederic Remington was a great artist or only an excellent draftsman is still going on. It is an idle controversy, really. Whatever the critics decide, no one can take away his unique contribution to America—his vast and detailed pictorial history of the West as it used to be, of the West as it lives on in the dreams of young and old alike the world over.

Further note for Philatelists. The ten-cent stamp in the Famous American Series was not the first time that Remington had been featured on a postage stamp. In 1897 John A. Merritt, then Third Assistant Postmaster General, wrote to Theodore Roosevelt for suggestions for their Trans-Mississippi Issue. Roosevelt made four suggestions: one of Remington's Cheyenne warriors in full war dress and eagle-feather bonnet; an oldtime Rocky Mountains or plains hunter and trapper, also to be reproduced from Remington; a Remington cowboy; and finally an emigrant wagon or prairie schooner (by Remington), though he admitted that it might be too much for the size of a postage stamp. Actually the Postmaster took the last suggestion, and an eight-cent stamp was issued in 1898, picturing troops convoying an emigrant train of covered wagons, a reproduction of a Remington painting.

In the same year was issued a fifty-cent stamp, "The Gold Bug," showing an old prospector with two pack mules on the desert, probably the result of Fred's own brief prospecting experiences. The same scene was also reproduced as a two-dollar stamp, with the title of "Harvesting in the West."

SELECTED BIBLIOGRAPHY

Books:

Bigelow, Poultney. *Seventy Summers.* 2 vols. Longmans, Green & Co., N. Y. 1925.

Card, Helen L. *The Collector's Remington.* Privately printed, Woonsocket, R. I., 1946.

Davis, Richard Harding. *Cuba in War Time.* R. H. Russell, N. Y., 1898.

Harper, J. Henry. *The House of Harper.* Harper & Brothers, N. Y., 1911.

Leigh, William R. *Western Pony.* Harper & Brothers, N. Y., 1933.

McCracken, Harold. *Frederick Remington, Artist of the Old West.* J. B. Lippincott Company, Philadelphia, 1947.

Remington, Frederic. *Pony Tracks.* Harper & Brothers, N. Y., 1895.

—— *A Roger's Ranger in French and Indian Wars.* Harper & Brothers, N. Y., 1897.

—— *Crooked Trails.* Harper & Brothers, N. Y., 1898.

—— *Sundown Leflare.* Harper & Brothers, N. Y., 1899.

—— *Stories of Peace and War.* Harper & Brothers, N. Y., 1899.

—— *Men with Bark On.* Harper & Brothers, N. Y., 1900.

—— *John Ermine of the Yellowstone.* The Macmillan Company, N. Y., 1903.

—— *Done in the Open.* (Folio of pictures with introduction and verses by Owen Wister) P. F. Collier & Son, N. Y., 1902.

—— *The Way of an Indian.* Fox, Duffield & Co., N. Y., 1906.

Rogers, W. A. *A World Worth While.* Harper & Brothers, N. Y., 1922.

Letters of Theodore Roosevelt. Selected and Edited by Elting E. Morison. Harvard University Press, Cambridge, Mass., 1951.

Taft, Robert. *Artists and Illustrators of the Old West: 1850-1900.* C. Scribner's & Sons, N. Y., 1953.

Thomas, Augustus. *Print of My Remembrance.* C. Scribner's & Sons, N. Y. 1922

Walsh, Richard J. *The Making of Buffalo Bill.* Bobbs-Merrill Co., Indianapolis, 1928.

Periodicals:

Collier's. September 17, 1910. "A Page from the Boyhood of Frederic Remington," By Orin Edson Crooker.
March 18, 1905. "The Remington Number."

Country Gentlemen. September, 1947. "Painter of the Rip-Roaring West" by Mrs. Myra Lockwood and Robert Taft.

Harper's Monthly. January, 1893. "Why We Left Russia," by Poultney Bigelow.

December, 1893. "An Outpost of Civilization," by Frederic Remington.

February, 1894. "In the Sierra Madre with the Punchers," by Frederic Remington.

March, 1894. "A Rodeo at Los Ojos," by Frederic Remington.

December, 1894. "An Arabian Day and Night," by Poultney Bigelow.

Harper's Weekly. December 6, 1890. "Chasing a Major-General," by Frederic Remington.

January 24, 1891. "The Sioux Outbreak in South Dakota," by Frederic Remington.

January 31, 1891. "Lieutenant Casey's Last Scout," by Frederic Remington.

September 3, 1892. "Buffalo Bill's Wild West Show in London," by Frederic Remington.

International Studio. February, 1923. "Remington at Twenty-three," by Mrs. Nellie Hough.

New York Public Library—*Bulletin.* August, 1940. "Frederic Remington," by Alvin H. Sydenham.

Outing. May 1887. "Coursing Rabbits on the Plains," by Frederic Remington.

Pearson's. October, 1907. "Frederic Remington," by Perriton Maxwell.

INDEX

186

187

188

189

192